PEACE IN OUR CITIES: RABBIS AGAINST GUN VIOLENCE

Second Edition

Edited by Rabbi Menachem Creditor

Second Edition

ISBN: 1482333813
ISBN-13: 978-1482333817

An act of violence is an act of desecration.

To be arrogant toward man is to be blasphemous toward God.

RABBI ABRAHAM JOSHUA HESCHEL
"*Religion and Race*"
January 14, 1963

RABBIS AGAINST GUN VIOLENCE

CONTENTS

FOREWORD

VIOLENCE, JEWS, AND JUSTICE

Rabbi Jill Jacobs

R. Meir said: When a human being suffers,
what does the [divine] tongue say?
My head is too heavy for Me,
my arm is too heavy for Me.
—Mishnah *Sanhedrin* 6:5

God is suffering. Every year, more than 31,000 Americans die by gunfire. Many of these die by their own hand; others are murdered by spouses, partners, family members, friends, or strangers. Were it not for easy access to firearms in a moment of crisis, many of these victims might still be alive.

The core Jewish teaching about humanity is that every human being is created in the image of God. For this reason, "one who sheds blood is regarded as though he had diminished God's likeness."[1]

Unfortunately, in our society, human life has become cheap. Political disputes and financial interests have gotten in the way of fulfilling our most basic societal obligation—keeping each other safe. Gun violence has become so routine, that the news of another suicide, another murder, or another accidental death hardly registers. Instead, we should view each one of these tragedies as an irreversible diminishment of the presence of the Divine.

Jewish law recognizes weapons as sometimes necessary instruments of war, but cautions against forgetting the context to which these weapons belong.

---

[1] Genesis Rabbah 34:14

Rabbi Joseph Caro, one of the most important medieval authorities, forbade bringing long knives into a synagogue because "prayer lengthens human life and a knife shortens it."[2] In the twentieth century, Rabbi Eliezer Waldenburg extended this prohibition to guns, whether displayed openly or concealed, except in a time of immediate danger.[3] Waldenburg clarified that instruments of war have no purpose outside of their intended context.

Our society seems to have forgotten this basic lesson. Guns, sadly, are still needed for warfare, but should never become commonplace in our homes. Just as we may not bring weapons into our prayer space, we also should not venerate guns, or become desensitized to their danger.

Our primary responsibility as human beings is to ensure the dignity and safety of other human beings. Every time a person dies by gunfire, the divine image is diminished, and God suffers.

---

[2] Beit Yosef, Orach Chayim 151

[3] Tzitz Eliezer 10:18

INTRODUCTION

SEEK THE PEACE OF THE CITY: THE MORAL MANDATE FOR GUN CONTROL[4]

Pastor Michael McBride

The prophet Jeremiah told the weary and heart-broken exiles of Jerusalem that they should "seek the peace of the city." Jeremiah's words ring in my ears as I reflect on our current national debate on gun violence. As a country, we stand on the edge of the most important opportunity we have had in over a decade to enact common sense gun laws and to address public safety. Yet, there is a deafening silence in this conversation.

To truly "seek the peace" of our cities and prevent gun violence, we must talk about urban gun violence and what works to prevent it. Failure to address this everyday issue is a moral abomination for anyone who takes the words of Jeremiah seriously.

Two years ago, I presided over the funeral of Larry, a teen from my congregation shot and killed in the Bay Area. More than 500 grief-stricken teenagers filled the pews that day. I asked how many of them had been to more than one funeral. Far too many hands went up. I kept counting. Three funerals? Four? I got as high as 10, and more than half of the young people in the church wept as their hands remained lifted in the air.

Jeremiah asks us to seek the peace of the city. There has been much conversation over the past week about a comprehensive plan to

---

[4] A version of this introduction appeared as "*The Moral Mandates of Gun Control*" in the Washington Post on January 14, 2013.

prevent gun violence. We've heard important and necessary calls for better enforcement of existing gun laws, an assault weapons ban, universal background checks and increased mental health investments. Even the nonsensical calls of NRA lobbyists to arm teachers have risen into the national conversation. Yet, there is a troubling absence of any mention of a targeted approach to addressing urban gun violence in our cities.

Let's be clear: Gun Violence is a concentrated problem that disproportionately impacts poor neighborhoods. Addressing it will require common-sense gun laws, along with a well-resourced and targeted response to particular cities.

Studies repeatedly show that a collection of best practices – including intentional collaboration between law enforcement, clergy, health workers, family members and formerly incarcerated individuals– that focuses on the less than 1 percent of the population who commit more than 60 percent of the gun crimes can create a sharp decline (decreases of more than 35 percent) of shootings and gun-related murders in the short term.

Yes, we need an assault weapons ban. *Yes,* we need universal background checks. *Yes,* we need mental health investments. But that by itself is insufficient. Any comprehensive plan to combat gun violence must include targeted urban violence prevention polices.

There are already numerous models the Administration could choose from such as the highly acclaimed Boston Ceasefire program.[5] This program teams police with numerous community organizations and churches to discourage gun carrying and spread the word among gang members about increased enforcement. According to the U.S. Department of Justice, in its first year alone, the Ceasefire program remarkably reduced gun violence by 68 percent.

We have a moral duty to act. We know what works to reduce gun violence, we know where it is most concentrated, and we know whom it most hurts.

The greatest moral failure of our time could be our inability to do what we know works to save the lives of young and poor people in cities across the country.

---

[5] Learn more at http://www.ncjrs.gov/pdffiles1/nij/188741.pdf

A Letter that Changed My Life

Rabbi Joseph B. Meszler

I received the following letter in anticipation of the Million Mom March, which later took place on Mother's Day, May 14, 2000. I was then serving at Washington Hebrew Congregation. Our synagogue bussed congregants there and joined the estimated 750,000 people who marched on Washington for better gun legislation.

While the march brought many people together, it did not produce any change in policy. More than a decade later, the fact we are stagnant on this issue is astounding.

The utter lack of change since then stands as an accusation to me and all of us that we have "stood idly by while our neighbor bleeds."[6] I read this letter every year with my students in an act of education and protest.

> Dear Rabbi,
>
> Nate and I are by nature not marchers. We do not enjoy crowds, preferring to promote causes privately. Almost in spite of ourselves, this year's Million Mom March will be an exception.
>
> In 1983, our first child, David, was shot and killed by another child. It was an accident that we have never been able to move beyond. For 17 years, our lives have been shaped, in a way deformed, by that event. It has hurt our souls, our marriage, our subsequent

[6] Leviticus 19:16

children, our families and our friends. It becomes a barrier between us and those who do not know because it is so difficult to say that there was a child who is not here anymore.

People are kind but unless you explain they do not understand. There is no polite way to say that we had a beautiful, bright 22-month old baby whose babysitter loved him very much but they kept a gun for protection and one day their four year old son found the gun and accidentally shot David through the head and killed him.

We really feel uncomfortable sharing that story because although we have been over every nuance for so many years, it is always a shock to bring it up. But there is no way we can go out for a meal on Mothers' Day and know that others have given up their Sunday and we have not. So we will both be at the March and hope that you understand that if only there had been a safety mechanism on that gun, David would still be with us.

Our hope is that you will think about us, and about David, and give thought to what it means to make our children safe through gun legislation.

Eve Wallace

I marched with this family and many others then, and I have joined efforts to pressure our government into better gun control since. I stand ashamed of our society that this epidemic continues unabated.

"AND NONE SHALL MAKE HIM AFRAID": THE JEWISH LEGACY AND GUNS

Rabbi Steven Greenberg

My mother and aunt were awakened in the middle the night. It was April, 1942. Armed French soldiers took my grandfather from his bed to the internment camp in Drancy. Two months later he was transported from Drancy on the outskirts of Paris to Auschwitz and was gassed there a month later.

After my grandfather was taken, my grandmother moved in with her friend Berthe, and the two women hid with their children in small attic apartment because the landlady couldn't bear to turn them away. A few months later, when the Nazis came searching for Jewish women and children my aunt was playing in the courtyard with Berthe's son and seeing the scene, the French barber in the corner apartment grabbed the two children crying for their mothers. "Come to Papa," he said, saving both them along with the women hiding upstairs who would have been exposed. The German soldiers continued upstairs. A stroke of ingenuity brought the land lady to serve the tired soldiers sausage, cheese and wine on the staircase leading to the last apartment. The interruption of food and wine distracted the men from their affairs and they did not continue their search after the meal. The barber and the landlady were just two of the many neighbors and strangers that saved my mother and aunt's lives. None of this resistance to Nazi aggression required a firearm.

These familial stories and their relationship to guns have been on my mind for the past four months.

This past January I joined a group of clergy visiting Washington, to engage the White House on the issue of gun violence in America. It was a moving experience that supported my sense that there was work to do to push America in the right direction on this issues, and I hoped that the organized Jewish community, being left leaning, could help. When I returned, I was shocked to discover how ambivalent the American Jewish Community was and still is on guns. More importantly, I discovered that in my own family there was a mixed response to the ideas that were proffered by the President in February. Why, I thought, should there Jews be in league with the NRA...in my family?

We were raised on the notion that the Jews are a gentle, non-violent people. Essau hunted; Jacob cooked lentil stew in his tent. Abraham, who famously took up arms to save his nephew Lot, did so with regret and shame. The military prowess of Joshua, David and Judah Maccabee was minimized by the rabbis, who had been traumatized by the Temple's destruction and the failed Bar Kochba rebellion that followed. For two millennia, violence belonged to Rome (representing the non-Jewish world) and resistance to the empire was embodied not in armed rebellion, but in the teaching of Torah.
This centuries old non-violent Jewish spirit was deeply challenged in the aftermath of the Holocaust. While even in late 19th century there was already a growing sense that Jewish passivity in the face of aggression was shameful, Jewish powerlessness began to feel morally irresponsible after Auschwitz. For many Jews, the military self-reliance of Israel was not only a revival of a long forgotten Israelite identity, but also a moral calling to never again trust others with our physical security.

My father bought a firearm in the 1968, a year after the Six-Day War. He claims to have done this out of a mix of family security and Jewish pride. For my father and many others, the "never again" sensibility that followed the Holocaust was given a fresh sense of energy and realism after the miraculous Israeli military success of the Six-Day War. Buying a gun was a way to join, if only in spirit, the brave soldiers who liberated the Kotel and reunited Jerusalem. A decade later my uncle did the same upon the urging of a son. Uncle Ron put it very clearly, "We are not going to go quietly this time."

There was another reason that guns became attractive to Jewish men. The recovery of a Jewish masculinity, even if only symbolically, was intoxicating. The image of the bespeckled, frail Jewish male became a foil to the muscular, tanned Israeli soldier with a rifle slung over his shoulder.

I shot my first firearm when I was twenty. In the middle of college I spent two years in an Israeli Yeshiva and had to participate in guarding the settlement at night. The training that Americans received was little more than a few hours of gun care and target practice. Armed with military grade rifles, we walked in pairs around the fenced border. It was exciting to be included (rather recklessly) in the very manly security detail on the periphery of the new self-reliant Jewish culture. I was unaware at the time how problematic this Israeli machismo would prove to be. Guarding a Jewish settlement with an M16 was part of my sense that from the ashes of Auschwitz, phoenix-like, we had returned. I also remember that a weapon is always firing, always shaping the fantasy of its use, looking for excuses. The weapon I carried silently intimated to me that hidden among the quiet slopes of the Judean hills were a million terrorists. A gun always means "I am not safe."

Latter day Jewish gun enthusiasts have the illusion that civilian guns would have made a difference in the Holocaust. While NRA Jews and others claim that Hitler disarmed civilians, it is just not true. More importantly, had my grandfather had a gun in Paris, he would have been no match for the French police force sent to arrest him. To use a gun at that moment would have been suicide. The notion that a gun would somehow have served him well is a disgrace to his memory and that of millions of Jews.

On the other hand, passivity in the face of aggression is not morally superior to self-defense. For the Israelis who defended themselves during the War of Independence against the combined forces of their Arab neighbors, weapons were a matter of life and death. Their need for weapons was not personal, as it is for so many Americans, but collective and essentially national. Perhaps this too is a distinction that matters. Gun ownership is complicated in America due to the strained nature of our social contract. Israelis have national enemies. They do not generally own guns to protect themselves from other Israeli citizens and certainly not from their own government. The glut of personal weapons in America appears then as a symptom of a much more troubling social unraveling that leads citizens to fear their own elected officials and ordinary neighbors to fear each other.

My father no longer owns a gun because he doesn't believe that having one is a benefit. My uncle not only kept his gun, but he purchased one for my aunt as well. In each bed stand there is a revolver. Uncle Ron still feels that having it there ready to use makes him more secure. Aunt Gloria is not so sure. While she has a great eye and when she goes shooting she can nail a bulls eye, she claims to own her firearm very reluctantly.

So given my familial, historical, religious and personal narratives, here is what I have come up with.

A Gun is a Dangerous Dog. The Talmud teaches that one should not keep a dangerous dog, a wild animal or wobbly ladder in one's house. They learn this from the verse "You shall bring not blood upon your house."[7] When you build a new house, you are to make a parapet around your roof so that you may not bring the guilt of bloodshed on your house if someone falls from the roof. Having a killing machine in your home is not advisable because accidents happen. However, if you must, then take precautions.

Since guns have immense power to protect and to destroy life it matters a great deal why you have a gun and what you are expecting to do with it. If your reasons are for hunting or sport, then your weapon does not need high capacity magazines nor does it need to be automatic. As well, weapons for sport do not need to be easily accessible and so they are best kept under lock and key.

Since a weapon kept for protection by definition needs to be ready to use, your reasons for harboring an easily accessible loaded gun must always out way the dangers. Owning a firearm in America increases your chances of dying by gun violence, by nearly three times! Angry domestic partners, family members not familiar with firearms and

[7] in Deuteronomy 24:8

clinically depressed people are given too easy a route to act rashly and irrevocably. That is why it is crucial to know if the dangers that concern you are real or imagined.

If your job involves carrying precious jewels down Fifth avenue you may reasonably want to own a gun. As an ordinary home owner, your inflated fears are very likely making you less safe. Using a gun, under pressure, often in the dark, is something people train for. Ordinary citizens are much more likely to hurt themselves or their family members than to save the day as they hope they will.

Weapons May Be Necessary; But They are Not Beautiful. In the Talmud there is an argument between Rabbi Eliezer and the sages.[8] Eliezer says that a weapon is an adornment for a man but the rabbis say, it is merely shameful. As it is said: "And they shall beat their swords into ploughshares, and their spears into pruning hooks."[9] Lethal weapons should not be loved or venerated but used responsibly for defense. For the hundreds of family members of the victims of Columbine, Virginia Tech, Grand Rapids, Carson City, Aurora, Oak Creek, Newton and more than 20 other such shooting since 1984, guns are not beautiful. For the family members of the nearly 30,000 people, many of them under the age of 20, killed by firearms yearly, guns are not beautiful.

Fear is a Curse. While no one should prohibit a law abiding citizen from obtaining a gun, as a society we ought to work very hard to change the culture that breeds such fear that people feel the need to buy weapons. Not surprisingly, the more weapons, the more fear, the more everyone feels the need to possess a weapon. Fear is the gun industry's best sales agent. The only beneficiaries of this escalating proliferation of fear and firearms are the gun makers whose wanton greed is partially to blame for our current crisis. Too many elderly people are afraid to be alone in their homes and too many of our youth are afraid to walk to school not knowing if they will get caught in the cross fire of some gun battle. These are not problems born or solved in day, but more guns will not make our homes, schools or our streets safer.

There is a sense that many people have that once the genie has been

---

[8] Babylonian Talmud, Shabbat 63b

[9] Micah 4:3

let out of the bottle, nothing can put it back. The county is awash in firearms. Given that reality, some say gun laws are actually too little too late. Perhaps it is true that the effect of gun laws will take a number of years to make a difference, but surely that is no reason not to act.

Beyond their immediate aims, laws are a means of cultural and educational direction. They communicate our values. Whatever gun laws we eventually pass will surely need to be joined with economic, cultural, religious and political efforts that include non-violence education and investment in schools, jobs creation, gun buyback options, clergy campaigns and partnerships between civil society and government to be truly effective.

Freedom from fear is the foundation of all blessings and the sign of a cursed culture is constant fear. At the end of the Book of Leviticus, when the blessings for keeping the covenant and the curses for violating it are pronounced, the curse that appears at the end of the list is fear. The remnant "will be pursued by the sound of a wind-blown leaf, and flee as if it were a sword; they will fall when no one pursues."[10]

Once fear replaces trust, every man feels the need to defend his turf. When fear rules, communities fragment, the life of neighbors becomes a threat, gangs grow in order to provide personal safety and guns becomes an entrance ticket to a life lived in violent competition for smaller and smaller scarce scraps of power and money. Fear unravels the social cohesiveness of any society to the point where a scared six grader in Queens can bring a loaded gun to school for "protection."

Gun control legislation has nothing to do with the sportsmen who hunt. The legislation is all about the dangers of fear. It addresses the ability of civilians to easily purchase military grade assault rifles and high capacity magazines and to have access to purchase handguns without background checks out of trumped up threats and exaggerated anxieties. The resistance to such sensible gun laws are all justified only by fantastical nightmares supported by imagined rather than real dangers. It is time to end this blight, the curse that

---

[10] Leviticus 26:36

brings blood on our house, that harbors danger parading as protection and that covers willful greed in a cloak of patriotism. American culture was famous for its hallmark of personal responsibility and neighborly care which together are the greatest protections against aggression and violence.

Micah's vision of beating swords into ploughshares ends with the banishment of fear, each one resting in ease under a fig tree with none to make them afraid. Until the messianic age there will be moments when life is defended by strong and brave soldiers wielding weapons. But the true life-affirming protection rests not in pistol in our hands, but in our trust of each other and in the neighborly care that over and over again, saved my mother, without a bullet.

Where is Our Strength? Bearing Arms in Jewish Thought

Rabbi Sheldon Lewis

Is there any people on earth that knows more deeply threats to its existence than the Jewish people? Is there any other people who have more frequently faced the danger posed by force of arms and the need to defend itself with weapons? It is this history of violent conflict that has provided the platform for musings by uncounted sages on the place and dangers of lethal arms in our lives. With the future prophetic vision of a world with weapons transformed into life-affirming instruments seemingly so far off, how can a human being live in real time within a world bristling with ever more deadly weapons and not be transformed and diminished by their presence? How can one cling to peaceful visions in an environment filled with assault weapons and high capacity magazines? We urgently need the wisdom of our forebears.

In a provocative Mishnah from two millennia ago, the rabbis struggled with this issue:

> A man may not go into a public domain [on the Sabbath] with a sword, a bow, a shield, a lance, or a spear; if he did so, he must bring a purification sacrifice. Rabbi Eliezer said: They are ornamental for a man. But the sages said: They are demeaning to him, for it says: "and they shall beat their swords into plowshares, and their spears into pruning hooks: nation shall not lift up sword against nation, neither shall

they learn war anymore."[11],[12]

The argument between Rabbi Eliezer and the sages is whether or not deadly weaponry can ever be considered as an ornament, as a normal part of one's garments. On Shabbat, jewelry for example can be worn and carried from place to place without violating the prohibition against work because they are considered ornamental. Rabbi Eliezer would extend this exemption to weapons. In his view, they are to be seen as part of one's clothing, analogous to a decorative bracelet or necklace. For the majority of sages, however, a sword and a shield can never be considered normative. In fact they are אינן אלא לגנאי. They are ever demeaning, shameful for a human being. And they are shameful in light of the dreams of a weaponless world. They may be necessary to defend life and limb, but no one should forget their place pitted against hoped for visions of peace. A weapon represents a deadly threat against other creatures. Even if one must master a weapon and use it when needed, the wise rabbis of the Mishnah argue against forgetting that they demean us. They dishonor the hopes for what a human being can be.

In fact, this Mishnah speaks here to a strategy for living in a dangerous real time. At least one day each week, on Shabbat, one retreats to one's more eternal values. Whatever six days of the week might bring, during the hours of Shabbat, one tries to enter an imagined future era in which one lives peacefully with every other creature. In addition to deepening bonds within a family and community, an observant Jew is enjoined to respect the life of even a pesky mosquito and never to pluck a flower from its plant or a leaf from a tree. Future visions are acted out in an imperfect world. Putting aside one's weapons is just one dimension of remembering clearly who one is.

Who are we really? In an insightful 14th Century comment, Rabbenu Bachya ben Asher, reinterprets Jacob's blessing of his son Judah near the end of his life. Jacob's blessing reads:

> Judah, you shall your brethren praise; your hand shall be on the neck of your enemies; your father's sons shall bow down before you. Judah is a lion's whelp; from the prey, my son, you have gone

---

[11] Isaiah 2:4

[12] Mishnah, Shabbat 6:4

> up. He stooped down, he couched as a lion, and as a lioness; who shall rouse him up? The scepter shall not depart from Judah, nor the ruler's staff from between his feet, as long as men come to Shiloh; and unto him shall the obedience of the peoples be. Binding his foal unto the vine, and his ass's colt unto the choice vine; he washes his garments in wine, and his vesture in the blood of grapes; His eyes shall be red with wine, and his teeth white with milk.[13]

Rabbenu Bachya comments:

> If you look at this passage, you will find in the blessing of Judah all of the letters of the *aleph-bet* written except the letter *zayin*. And the reason is: the victory of the kingdom of Israel, stemming from Judah, will not essentially emerge through weapons [*kle zayin*] like other nations. For the sword was the heritage of Esau, but the kings of Israel "will not inherit the land by agency of their sword."[14] [With them] the natural law and the force of the hand are not operative. Rather in accordance with merit and punishment, with the power on high of God, may He be blessed, [Israel will be victorious].[15]

Judah became the progenitor of the Jewish people. With one thoughtful expression from his pen, Rabbenu Bachya transforms a text from antiquity. The essence of Jewish destiny can never be achieved by means of weapons but rather from moral achievement. His reading raises up and reinterprets an ancient triumphal text and serves as a reminder of higher goals.

Perhaps the most powerful teaching I have found about the danger of weapons to those who bear them comes from the modern period. Rabbi Aaron Samuel Tamaret lived in the late 19th- early 20th centuries mostly in the Ukraine. He lived through the terrors of the Russian Revolution and World War I, and he became an eloquent teacher of non-violence in solving perplexing conflicts. In the following passage, he offers his remarkable view of events during the night of the tenth plague in Egypt:

> Now obviously the Holy Blessed One could have given the children of Israel the power to avenge themselves upon the Egyptians, but

13 Genesis_49:8-12

14 Psalms 44:4

15 Rabbenu Bachya, 14th Century, commenting on Genesis 49:8–10

> God did not want to sanction the use of their fists for self-defense even at that time; for, while at that moment they might merely have defended themselves against evildoers, by such means the way of the fist spreads through the world, and in the end defenders become aggressors. Therefore the Holy Blessed One took great pains to remove Israel completely from any participation in the vengeance upon the evildoers, to such an extent that they were not permitted even to see the events. For that reason midnight, the darkest hour, was designated as the time for the deeds of vengeance, and the children of Israel were warned not to step outside their houses at that hour – all this in order to remove them totally and completely from even the slightest participation in the deeds of destruction, extending even to watching them.[16]

Rabbi Tamaret offers a radically different view of why the Jewish people were ordered to stay indoors on that violent night. Their cause in seeking liberty was just; but, had they become the agents of violence that night, their power could later have been easily distorted and exercised in an unjust cause. Even witnessing violence could have dangerous implications for their future.

Rabbi Tamaret teaches us the insidious effects of bearing arms even when they are needed. A weapon carried and used can have a marked harmful effect upon its bearer. Even the sight of violence can scar a person and lead to harmful actions.

These rabbinic texts seem very contemporary. The violence around us caused most often by powerful guns represents great dangers both for potential victims and for everyone who executes or even witnesses the carnage. Insightful teachers recognized the risks and remind us of the need to hold on determinedly to our precious visions of a world at peace by embedding those visions in holy time and by transmitting a Torah of reconciliation to ourselves and to our children. Teaching peace, urgently and inspirationally recorded in sacred texts, seems especially urgent in an era of violence.

---

[16] Rabbi Aaron Samuel Tamaret, 20th Century, "Liberty" in *Mussar HaTorah V'haYahadut*

I LIVE ON A QUIET TREE-LINED STREET

Rabbi Shalom Bochner

I live on a street where I pass kids and families
 and kindergartners on scooters every day.
I live on a street where I can walk my children
 to their elementary school.
I live on a street where I walk eight short blocks
 to the synagogue where I work.
I live on a street with people and houses
 of many different colors and ages.
I live on a street that would look right at home
 in a Rockwell painting.
I live on a street where I sometimes hear the sound
 of a gunshot.
I live on a street where I hear guns when I'm laying
 in bed trying to fall asleep at night.

I wonder where the sound is coming from.
I wonder who or what the bullet was meant for.
I wonder if one day a bullet could hit my house.
I wonder if one day a bullet could hit my...

When I was young I fired pretend guns at the towers
 holding up power lines.
When I was young I played with toy guns and drew pictures
 of weapons.
When I was young I went to a day-camp and shot
 a 22-gauge rifle at tin cans and targets.
When I was young the sidewalks were full of kids, families,
 and kindergartners.
When I was young I walked for miles and rode
 my bicycle for hours.
When I was young I thought my house was safe,
 my street was safe, my world was safe.

I don't understand how I should explain about guns
 and gangs to my own children.
I don't understand why I hear the sound of gun shots on my street.

I just don't understand.

BECOMING ACTORS

Rabbi Nina Mandel

On January 21, 2013, Hadiya Pendleton, a 15-year old, African-American high school student was in Washington DC. She was performing with her school's band and drill team at arguably one of the most symbolic Presidential Inaugurations in history. Not only was Barack Obama, a man of color, being sworn in for a second term, he was doing it on Martin Luther King, Jr. Day. Both his re-election and Hadiya's participation were a poignant coda to the slain civil rights leader's legacy.

One week later, more than 80 clergy leaders representing ministers, Catholic clergy, rabbis, and imams, were also in Washington DC to be briefed on the president's gun control proposals and to advocate for more aggressive interventions in urban areas where gun violence is more prevalent. While this group was petitioning for greater support, Hadiya Pendleton was shot dead on a playground in Chicago. Her death occurred just a block away from the office of one of the keynote speakers in the clergy group. Hadiya Pendleton was the 42nd victim of gun violence in Chicago since January 1st.

Elie Weisel, the noted Holocaust-chronicler, is often quoted as saying that during that catastrophic time, there were three kinds of people: victims, perpetrators, and bystanders. Because he is also a human-rights activist, he suggests that this formula be considered whenever we discuss a large scale, life-threatening crisis. Gun violence in America is a large scale, life-threatening crisis. Until we are able to recognize that Hadiya Pendleton's death requires the same amount of outrage and action as the recent horrific mass shootings, we are all, at best, simply bystanders.

Who are the victims? They are the more than 1,200 people who died a gun violence-related death in the United States between December 12, 2012 and January 12, 2013. They are the innocent children, women, and men in cities, in suburbs, and in rural areas that die because of a culture of violence that promotes guns as the first-line solution to any scale crisis. They are the people whose cries for help turn deadly because spottily regulated firearms are always close at hand. The victims are also the walking wounded who sustained permanent injury, and the children who live in areas where they are more likely to be killed by a gun than they are to graduate high school. They are the fathers and mothers who have buried not one, but two, three, or even all of their own children.

And who are the perpetrators?

The perpetrators are NOT law-abiding, responsible gun owners. They are NOT the individuals who support the 2nd amendment.

The real perpetrators, beyond the violent criminals who commit the crimes, are those who make money on the free trade of guns and prevent regulation because they don't want to lose money. They are the ones who believe that weapons designed for the theater of war can and should be modified to be used for "sport." The perpetrators are the state and federal lawmakers who block legislation that would allow individual records to be shared, records that could prevent guns ending up in the hands of criminals. They are the ones who interpret the right to bear arms as the right to be above the law and need for regulation.

> **The real perpetrators, beyond the violent criminals who commit the crimes, are those who make money on the free trade of guns and prevent regulation because they don't want to lose money. And we are the bystanders.**

And we are the bystanders: those of us who are horrified when the random, rare, mass-killing happens - wringing our hands and wracking our brains about why - but failing to bring the same concern to the daily individual shootings. We are the ones who believe that gun violence is only about gangs and cities, not about abusive husbands and suicidal children. The bystanders are the ones who think boys will be boys and make television ads for video games that portray real people gunning down computer generated assailants with the tag line "inside each of us is a warrior." Bystanders see the problem but believe nothing can be done about it.

I would like to suggest that there is one more category of people to add to Weisel's formulation—*the Actor*. The actor is the activist who calls her congressperson to support comprehensive gun control reform. The actors are the family members who speak out at funerals and rallies, sharing their pain and their loss and asking that the violence ends with their dead children. The local lawmakers who push for better education, better healthcare, and better services are the actors who know that gun violence is only a symptom of a deeply broken society in which mass incarceration is seen as most expedient way to deal with at-risk youth.

We believe that violence against an individual is violence against our Creator.

The clergy who gathered in Washington, DC are part of the Lifelines to Healing Campaign of the PICO National Network and we are also actors. We came from places like Chicago, Boston, and Baton Rouge, Oakland, New Orleans, Richmond, and even Sunbury, PA because we share the belief that violence against an individual is violence against our Creator. Because my brothers and sisters in faith are tired of presiding over five, ten, and more funerals a month for people killed by gun violence. Because we know that a broken society is one in which we fail to take care of our fellow citizens. The Hebrew word for peace is Shalom and shares the same root as the word for wholeness. No one can be at peace in a world where wholeness is denied. To that end, we created the following statement and delivered it to Vice President Joe Biden's office, in hopes that he will be an actor too:

We share in the outrage growing from every corner of our nation that we have abandoned our young people to the clutches of violence fueled by greed, fear and despair. We bear witness to the deep pain of our nation's people, whose loved ones are dying needlessly in our communities across the land, that our God commands we speak out about the sanctity of all life and affirm that all have the right to live in peace and safety. We further assert that people of faith everywhere are commanded by our God to work tirelessly and in coalition with one another across racial lines, class and place lines, age and gender lines to vigorously confront the proliferation and increasing lethality of guns in our neighborhoods and cities, towns and streets, malls and schools.

We affirm that every life is precious in the eyes of our Creator and our God has no pleasure in the death of anyone. We are committed to uniting around the common pain and loss of who have suffered in Newtown and New Orleans, Chicago and Columbine and Oak Creek and Oakland. We are committed through our work to heal the soul of a nation. We will be vigilant partners in the struggle to transform our communities from the valley of the shadow of death to the land of the living.

To this end, we seek:

1. Universal Background Checks for all gun sales
2. Ban on Assault Weapons and High Capacity Magazines
3. Investments in Mental Health and Public Health Support
4. Targeted Investments and Approaches from Federal Government in Urban Cities most impacted by gun violence

A PROPHETIC RESPONSE TO GUN VIOLENCE[17]

Rabbi Menachem Creditor

In this moment, what does God want of us?

What are we called to do in the face of great devastation, some of which receives our nation's attention, most of which doesn't? How can we, in our efforts to extend God's Healing to our sisters and brothers, address Gun Violence, a terrible tear in the fabric of our nation?

What is a Prophet? How does she hear the Divine Weeping and call all God's children to awareness and action?

Hear the call of Isaiah, who reminded us that God wants, more than anything else, for us to

> ...unlock the fetters of wickedness, untie the cords of the yoke, to let the oppressed go free, to break off every yoke. ...to share your bread with the hungry, and to take the wretched poor into our homes; When you see the naked, clothe him, and do not ignore your own brother.[18]

The great Rabbi Abraham Joshua Heschel lived this lesson well. He reminded us that human beings, living Images of God, must have prophetic faith. But the faith of a prophet, Heschel taught,

---

[17] This essay was first presented as part of the PICO Network *Lifelines to Healing* "Healing the Soul of American from Gun Violence" clergy gathering in Washington, DC on January 29, 2013.

[18] Isaiah 58:6-7

> ...does not mean... to dwell in the shadows of old ideas... [or] to live off an inherited estate of doctrines and dogmas. In the realm of the spirit, only [one] who is a pioneer is able to be an heir.[19]

The prophets are the ones who demanded justice in the world, starting with Abraham's challenge to God "Shall not the judge of all the earth do justice?"[20]

We must feel fiercely[21] like the Prophets of old. And, like the prophets, as today's prophetic witnesses, we must see no divide between the political and the spiritual, for a world without fierce feeling is a world without spirit, and a religious tradition with nothing to say to the world is no longer engaged in bringing God's world to a more blessed day.

A Prophet feels every death as her own. A Prophet writhes with God's Pain, their soul contorting in ways that make it hard to breathe.

It is possible to lose hope. This world gives little encouragement to hope. And that is why we do what we do, why we answer our call with all the ferocity we can muster. We will not "stand idly by while the blood of our neighbors"[22] continues to be spilled.

Say it with me a tragic litany: *Newtown. Aurora. Columbine. Tucson. Virginia Tech.*

But now acknowledge with me also: These massacres received national attention. But the three high school students shot this past Thursday in Albany, CA did not. Nor did the seven people killed and six wounded in gun violence this past Saturday in Chicago, including a 34-year-old man whose mother had already lost three other children to shootings.

A prophet does not feel for SOME of these. A Prophet feels every

[19] Heschel, *Man is Not Alone*, p. 164
[20] Genesis 18:25
[21] Heschel, *The Prophets*, p. 5
[22] Leviticus 19:15

death as her own. A Prophet writhes with God's Pain, their soul contorting in ways that make it hard to breathe.

I repeat: It is possible to lose hope. But we are not allowed. Hope is our call. Extending hope, enabling peace, offering prophetic witness to the awful events of our day and communicating, over and over and over and over and over that God's world deserves better than fear and greed. God's world depends upon the work our hands, to be friends and partners together, to engage with our elected officials and law enforcement and teachers and others, to notice the violence that doesn't get reported, to breathe in and breathe out and breathe in and breathe out. Because if we don't, less of God's Work gets done.

I say that there are those in our country to whom Jeremiah would say today:

> On your shirt is found the life-blood of guiltless poor. Yet in spite of all these things, you say 'I am innocent.'[23]

If we are to avoid complicity in the growing violence of our country, we must remain every vigilant as witness to "the callousness of man" and not allow our heart to do what it wishes, which would be to "obliterate the memories, to calm the nerves, and to silence our conscience."[24]

The Prophets call us:

> *Do Not Be Calm.*
> *Do Not Forget.*
> *Do Not Be Silent.*

Friends, given the pressure on us, on everyone, I invite you right now to take a deep breath. Allow your body to experience a little more air. Breathe it in. Remember your power, God's Spirit, of which we are each but fragments.

There is great fear on the part of some that any response to Gun Violence is a rejection of the Second Amendment of our Constitution. *Fear.* There are those whose very work is the proliferation of

---

[23] Jeremiah 2:14

[24] Heschel, *The Reasons for My Involvement in the Peace Movement*

weapons of war on the streets of our cities and across our great nation with one over-riding concern: profit. *Greed.*

And this heady cocktail of Fear and Greed makes our work as religious leaders difficult. But we know that sacred work is not easy work. We do not answer to Fear and Greed. And we are not going to respond with hate to fear and greed – that is the way to make the fear and greed ever-stronger. We're going to outlast them.

There are those who have said that any response to Gun Violence reduces the U.S. Constitution into a blank slate for anyone's graffiti. *Lies.* It is our shared belief in the possibility of this country, our commitment to a democracy of free women and men of every orientation and color in the rainbow that gives us the courage to bend the historical arc of this country once again toward justice.

We, faith leaders who call God with an infinite variety of Holy Names, are called in this moment to do sacred work and to weather the intense fear and greed in a moment of national fragility. We will face the deaths our country continues to endure at the hands of unfettered Gun Violence, at the hands of those who follow profit margins and ignore those marginalized by society.

We will face the deaths our country continues to endure at the hands of unfettered Gun Violence, at the hands of those who follow profit margins and ignore those marginalized by society.

Heschel taught us, in the name of the Prophets, that "the heart of human dignity is the ability to be responsible."[25]

We call upon each other and all who will listen to be strong and resolute. We will "walk humbly with God"[26] and we will refuse to ignore the suffering of God's children.

For while, as Heschel said, in a moral world, "some may be guilty, but

---

[25] Heschel, *Required: A Moral Ombudsman*, United Synagogue Review, Fall 1971
[26] Micah 6:8

all are responsible."[27]

And so we pray together, women and men of faith, recognizing that which we have in common

May our great nation be safe place, where "every person may lie down with no one terrifying them."[28]

May people of every faith – *and of no faith* – work together to make the necessary changes to heal our nation from the scourge of Gun Violence.

My fellow clergy, women and men who serve God by serving all People, may the passion of the Prophets infuse our work, our words, our deeds, our thoughts – *every fiber of our souls* - so that when we do speak, we can cry more freely with God's Holy Tears and feel strengthened through that fierce feeling.

May the Source of Life whose Spirit awaits realization in every human breath fill us with hope and sustained determination us as we seek an end to all this death in our land.

Amen.

---

[27] Heschel, *The Prophets*, xix
[28] Leviticus 26:6, paraphrased

THE NAME ON THE BULLET[29]

Rabbi Jack Moline

We've all shaken our heads at the rising number of murders in Southeast Washington this winter. There is a sameness to the reports, and we rarely pay attention to anything but the gory details. Lamont Willis was one of those victims. The vital statistics of his life are not much different than many victims. He was 18, black, not yet out of high school, a veteran of some minor legal scrapes. He grew up in Temple Hills. On the last night of his life, he was out with a friend. They went to see an acquaintance of the friend. Lamont was present as the other two got into an argument. The acquaintance pulled a gun. Lamont was the last one out the door.

Every victim is some mother's child.

As a congregational family, we've seen the good die young and the righteous wither. We have seen cancers ravage, hearts deteriorate, kidneys fail. Our sons have fallen in service to their country and some few have been in the wrong place when a car loses control or a building falls.

But this is a waste in the fullest sense of the word. This young man lost his life to the most common cause of death among young black men: gunshot. The Torah commands us that even in time of war we

[29] Sermon given February 24, 1988. Danuel Jackson z"l was the long-time and much beloved custodian of Rabbi Moline's synagogue.

are not to waste the fruitful trees, and this young man, looking to join the Marines, was cut down before he bore his fruit.

Every victim is some mother's child. It doesn't help to point a finger at environment or economics. It doesn't satisfy to cluck our tongues and dab our eyes. It doesn't ease the discomfort to say, "he wasn't one of ours."

That is because Lamont Willis was one of ours. He was Danuel Jackson's nephew, his sister's youngest.

Ribono Shel Olam, Master of the Universe, what are we to do?

UNNECESSARY DANGER: A JEWISH REFLECTION ON GUNS, VIOLENCE AND PERSONAL SAFETY[30]

Rabbi Aaron Alexander

There have been several important articles written in the last week using traditional Jewish sources to either support or subvert gun control. I would like to add to that discussion but in a slightly different way, explaining and interpreting an obscure, yet relevant, 18th century legal ruling.

The formidable traditionalist, Rabbi Ezekiel Landau (1713-1793, Prague), was once asked if it would be permissible, according to Jewish law, for an observant Jew to enter the forests and hunt - for sport - with a rifle.

Rabbi Landau argues that although there may not be an explicit violation of a legal principle - either animal cruelty or unnecessary waste - any Jew who hunts solely for pleasure is participating in something cruel and outside the boundaries of the Jewish ethical tradition. To be clear, he purposefully does not include killing an animal for safety and/or sustenance - an immediate need. But he is severely opposed to anything short of those two necessities.

The crux of Rabbi Landau's argument against hunting for sport, though, relies on a somewhat general teaching from the Bible: "*And*

[30] This essay first appeared on Rabbi Alexander's HuffPost blog on Dec. 21, 2012

you shall be very watchful of yourselves."[31] In other words, carefully guard your own safety and do not intentionally place yourself in danger without pressing need. Rabbi Landau contended that in order to hunt one must willingly enter places where there is risk present, in this case, the forest. While the modern sport of hunting may be less precarious, anyone who has hunted with Dick Cheney would have to agree that it isn't without potential harm.

He buttresses this argument using a biblical character, Esau. Rabbi Landau writes:

> And could one find a more qualified and expert hunter than Esau?! No! Yet the Torah teaches that Esau himself exclaimed about his life's profession, '*Here I'm going to die...*'[32] The text should be taken quite literally. Esau was frightened everyday lest he would meet death while out hunting. Therefore, if an expert like Esau both knew about and was scared of the real and present danger, how could a Jew place him/herself in this kind of situation when the only impetus for it is desire!?

Rabbi Landau's point, based on biblical narrative, should not be taken lightly. If even Esau was constantly aware of the potential and mortal danger, certainly any less proficiency than "expert" would demand a only severe and legitimate need to permit such a potentially harmful activity. At least according to the Jewish values that Rabbi Landau espoused.

And I think this ruling is useful in the conversation about Jews and guns. Why? Rabbi Landau articulated, through the prism of Torah values as he interprets them, that in the absence of a real-and-present need, some activities are too explicitly against some of our core values, like preservation of life, safety and the inherent holiness in all of God's creation. For a Jew to engage in them would be a violation of not only the Torah, but decency.

His position and arguments cause me to reflect on our current reality in several tangible ways.

There are, of course, times when we must (are obligated) insert ourselves into dangerous situations, and with weapons. We must

---

[31] Deuteronomy 4:15

[32] Genesis 25:32

also be well prepared for such events. Sometimes it is for a profession. Sometimes, sadly, war. Other times we must be ready and willing to protect the public.

But what about using and owning tools explicitly created for death in voluntary and recreational situations? What does Rabbi Landau offer us in answering that question for Jews interested in a perspective based in Torah?

Having guns is dangerous for those who own them as well as those who are around them. Nobody can argue with that. Sure, experts are safer. Then let's require our gun users/owners (i.e., those who need to have guns) to be actual experts. That includes proficiency in not only the wielding of the weapon, but also its safe storage.

> **in the absence of a real-and-present need, some activities are too explicitly against some of our core values, like preservation of life, safety and the inherent holiness in all of God's creation.**

Jews possessing guns for hunting? For just firing at the range for sport? Gun collecting? All of these create potent situations of danger and for no useful and life-affirming reason that can't be accomplished through another activity. Accidents with children/adults and guns are all too common and they can be prevented. But until safety is ensured, I cannot find a Jewish ethical justification for gun ownership that doesn't rely on food, clothing and/or self-defense.

I know there are plenty of hobbies out there that are fairly dangerous. I also think it is quite silly to compare bungee-jumping to shooting guns. But, theoretically, going to a gun range, renting a gun, firing it, and then going home is pretty benign. A safe gun range is just that – *safe* – statistics show. The guns don't need to go back to homes where there are children or other vulnerable people in harm's way. It is when guns leave the range that I am extremely wary and would like assurances that those who house them will be vetted and regularly tested in gun-storage safety.

Also, Rabbi Landau's principle of an act, which may not be explicitly forbidden based on clear legal principles, but, nevertheless, holding that it is still something we ought not do, influences me. There is something about firing a gun (which I have done) for recreation that rubs me the wrong way. Guns equal violence.

My advice: *find something else to do. Honestly.*

We live in a society in which the glorification and celebration of gun violence is ubiquitous. It has to end. It is a significant piece of the puzzle. Shooting guns for the sole reason of a rush, a game, a fun time, group bonding... If a Jew asked me if it is permissible, I would say no. To what end? Guns, really? I just don't see how an object that has been – and is still – wielded for so much violence and death can be used as a tool for pleasure without sending all the wrong messages and creating needless potential for harm. Shooting guns at a range to become an expert and potentially be able to save a life? If that is the goal I think it is different, and permitted. Even laudable.

This isn't to say that I think all possible dangerous activities are problematic. I know there are risks in countless activities that build character, create happiness and foster group development. They are all very much life-affirming activities. It isn't the ends that I stand against, but the particular means by which we achieve the ends. In this case, guns.

As a rabbi writing for those who live their lives with the Torah as a guidepost, know that I do not advocate Jewish gun owners simply giving up their weapons. I do, however, advocate keeping them in the hands of those expertly trained to a) use them, b) store them safely and c) use them only when there is a clear and necessary purpose.

Let's all continue to pray for all those in need of comfort. Let's unite in building a safer world. Let's do this together, one sensible decision at a time.

ANSWER OUR PRAYERS: REMARKS AT THE NATIONAL CATHEDRAL GUN VIOLENCE VIGIL[33]

Rabbi Julie Schonfeld

All of God's children are born with eyes at full size.

This is how the Creator assures that our babies will be irresistibly beautiful to all of us and that adults will protect all of our young.

Last Thursday night, I brought my first grader, Gabriel, to a holiday party in Washington where he hoped to shake the President's hand. He was one of the first to arrive and spent the whole evening at the rope line, waiting to fulfill the fantasy that all little boys and girls share in this great country. I told Gabriel that there are millions of children in America and that we had done nothing to make us especially deserving of this privilege, but that from the gratitude that the Jewish people feel to live in America, he had a duty to bring the message of the future, the message of children, to Washington.

When the President finally came out a few hours later, he reached for the many outstretched hands behind me and above my head, and I

[33] Rabbi Julie Schonfeld spoke on December 21, 2012, at the National Cathedral Gun Violence Vigil, where leaders in the Jewish community joined together with Roman Catholics, Episcopalians, Muslims, Baptists, Methodists, Quakers, Evangelicals, Sikhs and other faiths to call for increased gun control.

– Mr. President, there's a little boy right here, resident, right down here, just want to make sure ittle boy.

Obama looked at me with a warm smile and said, "I never little kids, don't worry, I never miss 'em." My Gabriel, whom l Gabi, got his handshake.

ast Friday morning, still exhausted, Gabi fell asleep on the train lying on my lap at just about 9:30 and woke up when we arrived, insisting that we go to his school so he could tell his big brother and his teachers and his friends what he had done.

It was there, at about 12:30, with hundreds of children running past me for early dismissal before the Jewish Sabbath, and my children's beloved teachers coming over to give me a hug and kiss, that I got the first tweet of what had happened in Newtown.

All faiths share many things in common – one of them is a recognition of a certain type of religious experience, whether in joy or anguish when the boundaries between ourselves and other people melt away.

Such an experience I had, and my mind and heart cannot turn away from last Friday morning, spent with my first-grader, and his first grade. I cannot comprehend God's inscrutable presence in the world, but Judaism has reasserted for 3,000 years in the face of every tragedy that we are all God's beautiful children, and we are all responsible.

Americans are one people in one great country, and we are all the parents of all of our children.

I can only pray to God for the strength and courage to fulfill these responsibilities. A month before Yom Kippur, the solemn day of atonement, Jews begin to recite s'lihot, prayers that ask God's forgiveness for our sins. Jewish tradition teaches that we must first face ourselves and ask for God's forgiveness in order to fulfill our sacred duties, the most important of which is to protect the infinite sacredness of every human life.

One week later, I have come back to Washington, to bring not only to the President, but also to Congress, the message of my first-grader, the message of Gabriel, the message of children.

Across the aisle and across the country, we are the mothers and fathers of all of our children whom we must protect from the ravages of gun violence. Gun violence is taking a huge toll on our society, and the easy accessibility of firearms causes more people to be killed or injured than in any other developed country. While we continue to grieve for the families of those lost, we must also support our prayers with action. We should not allow this kind of firepower in our society.

- We must ban the sale of assault weapons
- We must institute appropriate background checks
- We must cease the online sale of ammunition

Join me, today, in signing the Jewish Council for Public Affairs' petition to end gun violence, so that as a united force, we can work together with local, state and national leaders to honor the victims while supporting comprehensive action and meaningful legislation.

The s'lihot, or forgiveness prayers, offer God our best reasons for why we deserve to be forgiven so that we may better do God's work. And so for centuries, we have called out to God with these words:

> Forgive us, O God.
> Do it, for the sake of the babies who were just weaned.
> Do it for the sake of the babies who are still nursing.
> Do it for the sake of the small children of the schoolhouse
> who have never sinned.
> Do it for your sake, O God.
> Save us.
> Save us and answer us.
> Answer our prayers today, for we live only to praise You.

TESTIMONY BEFORE THE MINNESOTA SENATE JUDICIARY COMMITTEE ON GUN VIOLENCE

(February 22, 2013)

Rabbi Michael Adam Latz

Mr. Chairman, thank you for inviting me today and for the honor for addressing the committee. For the record, my name is Michael Adam Latz and I am the Senior Rabbi at Shir Tikvah Congregation in Minneapolis. [I am, in fact, the chair's much younger cousin]. I'm here on behalf of my congregation, as well as Protect Minnesota, Jewish Community Action, the National Council of Jewish Women, and a diverse coalition of people of faith across the political spectrum seeking to end the scourge of gun violence in our cities and communities.

I am here, like so many others, because I know the cost of gun violence personally.

On July 28, 2006, a gunman stormed into the Jewish Federation of Seattle. Within a matter of nine minutes, he murdered Pam Waechter and shot five others: Layla, Carol, Cheryl, Christina, and Dayna Klein. Dayna was a congregant of mine and when the gunman appeared at her office door, he raised the gun to her chest and fired. Dayna, 37 years old and 17 weeks pregnant, instinctively raised her left arm, where the bullet entered on one side and exited the other, ricocheted off her thigh, and then burned a large hole in the carpet. Dayna, bleeding profusely, managed to call 911 and when the gunman returned and pointed the weapon at her face, in a moment that changed history, she handed him the phone and said, "CNN is on the line; they want to speak with you." He surrendered a few moments later.

I was amongst the first people to arrive at Harborview Medical Center after hearing about the shooting. Medical staff quickly brought me back to Dayna's room. I held her right hand, while doctors worked to save her left arm. The hole from the bullet was large enough for a small child to put her hand through; it haunts me every day.

I am here for Dayna and for Cheryl and to honor Pam Waechter's memory, for Princess' son Anthony, for the children of Sandy Hook and the kids of North Minneapolis and the Iron Range and Accenture Signage and so many more innocent souls whose shot up corpses litter the streets of heaven.

I am here as a rabbi, a man of deep faith, called to leadership by God and my community, to offer a vision of peace, transformation, equity, and justice.

I am here in the my most important role: as a father of young children, with the responsibility of raising them resting upon my shoulders every moment, and the dream of watching them grow up the guiding vision of mine and my husband's lives. What other purpose is there, what truly matters in this lifetime, when confronted with the joy, the agony, the exhaustion, and the privilege of raising up the next generation?

Before you, the elected leaders of this great state, rests legislation to do something to help end needless pain and suffering caused by gun violence.

There are those here who believe that if you can't do everything, without a perfect or comprehensive plan, somehow, you should do nothing; that, doing nothing is better.

Doing nothing is moral impotence.

Let us be guided by the wisdom of the great Talmudic sage, Rabbi Tarphon: Lo Alecha hamlacha ligmor, lo alecha ligmor. You are not required to complete the work, neither are you free to abstain from it. Our sages teach that if you save a single human life, you save the world.

We do not look to you, our elected leaders, to solve all our problems, to magically end gun violence.

We look to you to do your part, to guide a respectful debate, to remember that God gave us all two ears and one mouth—we'd all be the wiser to use them proportionately, and to enact legislation that helps.

We look to you to demonstrate moral courage; to join with us, the citizens of this great state, and do your part, to work with us to create a society of laws, where none shall be afraid.

Above all, let our solemn duty be to honor and to remember: The memories, the horror, the death, the agony of Columbine and Virginia Tech and Tucson and Aurora and Accenture Signage and Sandy Hook Elementary School are seared into our souls. May our legacy do justice to their lives, and our own.

Thank you, Mr. Chairman and members of this committee.

Be Like Busch: An Open Letter from Four American Rabbis to the NRA Membership[34]

Rabbis Aaron Alexander, Sharon Brous, Ronit Tsadok, and Menachem Creditor

Dear Average NRA Member:

I know it feels like we are worlds apart right now. But we both know that there is more that unites us than divides us.

We both love our country deeply.

We both celebrate and defend liberty, which stands at the core of our American ideal.

We both work hard -- really hard -- to protect the lives of those we love.

And here's what else we agree on:

We both recognize the absurdity of blocking background checks designed to keep deadly weapons out of the hands of violent

[34] This essay first appeared on Rabbi Alexander's HuffPost blog on April 23, 2013.

criminals and people with severe mental illness. We, like most Americans, think that high capacity magazine clips and assault weapons, designed only to maximize deadly impact, ought not be available to everyday folks like you and me and Adam Lanza. We know that about 90 percent of Americans -- including many members of the NRA -- support reasonable gun restrictions, just as there are reasonable restrictions on who and how one can get their hands on a driver's license or Sudafed.

The NRA leadership claims that their interest is in protecting the 2nd Amendment and representing its many members. But, as former NRA-member Adolphus Busch said just this week:

> The NRA appears to have evolved into the lobby for gun and ammunition manufacturers rather than gun owners.

And as gun-toting mama from Wyoming, Sarah Zacharias, recently wrote:

> I have not seen a gun sale that didn't seem worthy of a short background check, nor have I seen a sale impeded by that process. I have never seen any form of wild game hunted with one of the guns that was once banned under the previous assault weapons ban. I have never seen a sportsman with a magazine on his gun and I have never seen a competition shooter loaded down with more than a few bullets either... I betcha that if enough of us told the gun industry that we aren't spending more money until they drop the fallacious propaganda storm and start contributing to a meaningful gun responsibility conversation, that good, meaningful laws might come pouring out of the woodwork.

You have a voice. You, a gun owner and a member of the NRA, can speak to your leadership and demand they listen to you. You can speak to your senators and representatives and tell them that they were put into office not to cow to the pressure of lobbyists, but to represent the people. And the people have spoken.

The first question asked in the Bible is "Am I my brother's keeper?" The answer -- which echoes across the generations, cutting through all social, ethnic and communal borders -- is YES. We are our brothers' and sisters' and neighbors' keepers. We are our children's keepers.

We need to work together, you and me. This is not a red state/blue state issue. This is not even a Second Amendment issue. We don't want your guns. We do want to make our streets and schools and parks safe. For your sake. For our sake. For our children's sake. For the sake of our great country. Join us. Speak up.

Signed,

Your Unlikely Partners in Liberty and Safety
Rabbi Aaron Alexander, Rabbi Sharon Brous,
Rabbi Menachem Creditor, Rabbi Ronit Tsadok

ON THE SANDY HOOK SCHOOL TRAGEDY[35]

Rabbi Sam Weintraub

Over the past five days, we have gathered together and mourned the innocents who were killed at the Sandy Hook Elementary School. We have joined in services last Shabbat, in our homes and schools and work places, and in casual meetings on the street, to cry and pray together, and to comfort each other even as this tragedy defies understanding.

We have heard from our President and other political leaders a new resolve to address the deeper causes of gun violence in our country. That is very welcome news. I want us to move together as a country on this.

Generally, I try to keep my mind open to all points of view, but on the matter of gun control, I find it impossible to understand how anyone can support the status quo. The Harvard School of Public Health, in a recent study focusing on 26 developed countries, showed that the more firearms, the more homicides. Conversely, when strict controls were adopted, homicides drop markedly.

The massacre in Newtown has re-invigorated public conversation about gun violence, mental health and pubic security. This discussion—and more importantly concrete political decisions - are way overdue.

---

[35] This sermon was delivered at Kane Street Synagogue in New York on December 19, 2012.

We need more aggressive gun controls. To my mind, these should severely limit the amount of weapons an individual may possess, strictly monitor the possession and use of ammunition, require more extensive and lengthy background checks and regular follow up psychological and medical tests of gun owners, and the storage of many private weapons in locked areas under police supervision. Further, we need not only to remove stigmas from mental health diagnoses and treatment, but we must, as a society, institute regular mental health examinations for young people, until age 21, just as we encourage yearly physical exams or check their eyesight and hearing.

We must have to take the discussion deeper. Political reforms will not offer a panacea. Recall that, in the case of Adam Lanza, the guns were legally obtained, properly stored and used in legal, supervised sporting arenas. The Sandy Hook Elementary School had an updated security system, which Adam had to shoot through. While clearly troubled, several friends described Adam as the son of upstanding, respected, generous, affluent parents who apparently had sought treatment for him.

Do I mean that we should therefore suffer silently, and regard the loss of 26 precious souls as simply the price of our constitutional freedoms? Certainly not.

We must take the discussion deeper. That will involve, first, a new discussion about guns and their importance for Americans. Nancy Lanza, like millions of other Americans, seems to have valued her firearms not only for self-defense but for sport. What does it say about us as a society that lethal weapons are enjoyed so widely for their entertainment value? Israel, as even the casual tourist notices, is a country in which citizens are surrounded by automatic weapons. The tens of thousands of Israelis on active duty often keep their weapons with them, on and off base. However, in military training, Israelis learn "*Tohar Haneshek*" (purity of arms), a religious perspective which limits the use of guns only for the defense of life. As a result, the incidence of gun violence in the civilian sector is low, despite the ubiquity of weapons.

What does it mean to look deeper for the roots of gun violence?

I would like to share with you excerpts from an article written 41 years ago in the United Synagogue Review:

> Ten or twenty years ago no one would have believed that American boys could have acted in such a way. But they did. Who else is guilty? Who else is to blame? Did our religious leaders not fail to install in our people an absolutely, unconditional sense of horror for murder? Relativity of values, permissiveness, is today a powerful trend in living and thinking. This trend tends to become universal, embracing all thoughts and action. It may also embrace homicide or even genocide. There is one issue in regard to which no permissiveness or relativity must be tolerated and that is murder!...The sense of sanctity for human life is subsiding.... [36]

Rabbi Abraham Joshua Heschel z"l wrote these words in response to the controversial conviction in military court of Second Lieutenant William Calley, for leading his platoon in the "My Lai Massacre' of hundreds of unarmed South Vietnamese civilians on March 16, 1968.

Heschel then went on to offer a teaching he found in the Prophets of Israel, his now famous distinction between guilt and responsibility.

> Guilt ...implies a connection with or involvement in a misdeed of a grave or serious character, the fact of having committed a breach of conduct, especially such as violates law and involves penalty. ...Responsibility is the capability of being called upon to answer, or to make amends, to someone for something, without necessarily being directly connected with or involved in a criminal act.[37]

We are all innocent of the atrocities of December 14 in Newtown. However, according to Jewish ethics,

> one who can forbid his fellow citizens from committing a sin, but does not, is seized for the sins of his fellow citizens.[38]

Jewish law and tradition emphasize our responsibility and obligations to each other. Judaism encourages individual to be a proud, satisfied self, but also affirms that individuals develop and enhance personal identity mostly by being part of the larger reality

---

[36] Abraham Joshua Heschel, "*Required: A Moral Ombudsman*", United Synagogue Review, Fall 1971

[37] Ibid.

[38] Babylonian Talmud, Tractate Shabbat 54b

and moral purpose of a group.

In the context of the discussion about firearms, the Jewish emphasis on shared obligations offers important insights. Firearms must be appreciated for their effect on human life, not on their potential for amusement. We have to have a serious public discussion not primarily about the occasional mass or serial killer but about the thousands of American men and women who murder others and kill themselves with guns ever year.

What is in their hearts and minds? How did it get here? What relationships have they seen glorified on the screen? on the street? in the school yard? What have been the loudest voices during their youth and maturation? Was it the Were they ever exposed to a serious, influential educational track which taught nonviolence? What outlets were they given to deal with depression, anger or alienation? What training or encouragement were they given to be sensitive to the grandeur of God's creation, to cultivate a sense of wonder and gratitude for the simple gift of being alive?

In the context of the discussion about firearms, the Jewish emphasis on shared obligations offers important insights. Firearms must be appreciated for their effect on human life, not on their potential for amusement.

As human beings we have a desire not just to eat, to survive, and to enjoy sexual pleasure. We have ontological needs to pray, to wonder, to be grateful, and to experience moments of exultation. We need to feel that moments are unique and that we can do great things. To paraphrase Rabbi Heschel, we don't only need tranquilizers and sedatives. We also need stimulants. We are different than animals because we reject living on a level which is shallow and repetitious. We need to fashion our lives around the visionary and the ultimate, not just the practical and utilitarian.

There is no fairness or justice in the murder of the sacred souls in Newtown. But they will not have died in vain if, moved by this tragedy, we mobilize to prevent the murder of others and to actively teach the ways of nonviolence and cooperation.

May their rest be dignified and may their beauty and innocence turn us all to compassion and hope.

God relies on human beings to bring moral and spiritual light to our world. In the wake of this tragedy, if each of us can promote practices and policies of caring and understanding, then good will triumph over violence.

YOU SHALL NOT MURDER[39]

Rabbi Robyn Fryer Bodzin

On Wednesday, January 9, 2013, Toronto snowbirds Donny Pichofsky and his wife Rochelle failed to show up for a lunch date with a neighbor in south Florida.

The next day, according to a news report, at six-thirty in the evening, a friend with a spare key entered the townhouse to check on the couple.

The neighbor found Donny and Rochelle dead.

Shortly after the discovery, a spokesperson with the Hallandale Beach Police Department announced that the Canadian retirees had been murdered. No more information has been shared. This week, Hallandale police were furthering their investigation up in Toronto.

Donny Pichofsky was a real person. This is not a description of an episode of CSI:Miami or Law & Order. I have known the Pichofsky family my entire life. The Pichofskys have a summer cottage near my family summer home. As a little girl, I remember doing aerobics with Donny's first wife Sandy, z"l. Donny davened with my Zayda of blessed memory, every Shabbat morning during July and August for decades, at the little shul in Jackson's Point, Ontario.

[39] This sermon was delivered at of Israel Center of Conservative Judaism in New York City on February 2, 2013.

What I am trying to convey is that people I know were violently murdered. Murdered. Here, in these United States. In sunny Hallandale, Florida.

Donny and Rochelle's killer defied the words of God, the words of chapter twenty of sefer Shemot, which was read just this morning. Donny and Rochelle's killer broke mitzvah number six (out of the ten that were given during the revelation at Sinai).

לֹא תִּרְצָח
You shall not murder[40]

Lives are taken daily. Not by God, but by other people, multiple times each day in this country. They don't have that right.

On average, 33 mothers grieve each and every day in the United States, day in and day out, because their children lost their lives. And it is a *shundah* that we sing about living in the Land of the Free in our national anthem. Those of us who gather to *daven* together in this synagogue might not see it, because we live in relatively "good" neighborhood, but the United States is not a safe or free place to live. We lock our cars and front doors for a reason. Our computers have passwords for a reason; crime and violence.

Out of a population of 395, 317, Forbes magazine reports that Oakland, California has a crime rate of 1,683 crimes per 100,000 residents each year. Oakland's high levels of poverty and proximity to drug corridors combine to generate lots of violence.

Out of a population of 713,239, Forbes magazine reports that Detroit had a violent crime rate of 2,137 per 100,000 residents. Motown has become the most dangerous city in America.

Although Chicago has logged more homicides than any other U.S. city lately, (There were 42 as of January 31 for this new year) it does not have the highest homicide rate. That honor goes to New Orleans, whose murder rates was 32.65 per 100 000.

And New York, home to over 8 million people, only has 2.72 murders

[40] Exodus 20:13

per 100,000 residents.

We are all created equal, we are all created in God's Image, yet there are people out there who pick up a gun, and choose, as if it is their prerogative, to terminate the life of another person.

How many more stories do we need to hear until we say enough is enough?

For the media and for the White House, Newtown was the *ad kan*, the "enough", the spark that united the country into a national conversation about guns and violence in America.

There is just too much fear in this country.

While Newtown has become a catalyst for conversation and perhaps legislation, we have to remember that what happened in Newtown happens every day in America. That point was emphasized to me earlier this week.

As many of you know, I took the train to Washington DC on Monday morning. It was an honor to be invited to spend two days with a delegation of faith leaders, engaging in issues surrounding the epidemic of guns and violence in America.

Monday was a working day. We heard from experts and consultants, and I now know more about the history of guns than I ever thought I would need to know. We honed our joint, unified message throughout the day. We learned best practices from each other. We said "*Amen*" quite a lot, and the next day, Tuesday, was a presenting day.

While it felt a little unreal to be at the White House, the message that we conveyed to President Obama's Office and Vice President Biden's Office overshadowed any of the "I am at the White House" giddiness.

If you saw any of the pictures I posted on Facebook, you would see that there were not so many white folk at this convening. But it was important that white faith leaders were in attendance. We heard from our brothers and sisters in congregations who serve inner cities, who officiate at funerals for eighteen year olds and sixteen year olds who are killed by guns and gangs.

An understanding that I came away with from my time in DC is that there is just too much fear in this country.

A third grader at Daly Elementary School in Detroit brought a loaded gun to school last week and showed it to a classmate, who then told his mother. That mom called the school, and school officials searched the child and found a loaded gun. Sources say the eight-year-old told police he needed the gun for protection because he was being bullied. EIGHT YEARS OLD. PROTECTION FROM BEING BULLIED with a gun???

What were we doing when we were eight years old? What did we bring with us to school?

"It is possible to lose hope," writes my colleague Rabbi Menachem Creditor, "But we are not allowed. Hope is our call."

As modern Jews, we know about hope. It is the name of our Israeli national anthem, Hatikvah. The hope. In that anthem we say *lihyot am chofshi bartzeinu*, we hope to be a free people in our land.

Just as in Israel, so too in America.

We cannot and should not be paralyzed by fear. Nor can we say that since this violence is not happening in my neighborhood, then it is not my problem. In the words of Elie Wiesel, the opposite of love is not hate, it is indifference. And if we are being indifferent to the plight of fellow Americans who are being gunned down, then we spit in the face of Rabbi Akiva who said:

> You shall love your fellow as yourself.[41] This is a great principle in the Torah.[42]

While it is not in the Ten Commandments, Rabbi Akiva is right. It is a *klal gadol*, a great principle. We need to care for all people and find a place in our hearts to love all of God's people. Being Jewish, being a

---

[41] Leviticus 19:18

[42] Genesis Rabbah 24:7

light onto the nations means exiting our *dalet amot*, our four walls, and finding a way to care for all.

As we recite each Shabbat morning:

> We have not come into being to hate or to destroy. We have come into being to praise, to labor and to love.[43]

In our statement delivered both at the White House and in a press conference later that day we said:

> We are committed to uniting around the common pain and loss of those who have suffered in Newton and New Orleans, Chicago and Columbine and Oak Creek and Oakland. We are committed through our work to heal the soul of the nation.

As people of faith, when we talk about guns and violence, we have a moral imperative to include those people that the media forgets. As people of faith, we need to ensure that the hundreds of thousands, if not millions of young children growing up in our inner cities stop feeling as if they are living in the valley of the shadow of death, but rather can wake up every morning knowing they are in the land of the living.

It is with these thoughts at the forefront, that the clergy of the PICO National Network Lifelines to Healing Campaign asked for targeted investments and approaches from the Federal Government for Urban Cities most impacted by gun violence.

As people of faith, when we talk about guns and violence, we have a moral imperative to include those people that the media forgets.

Faith leaders, I learned, have a voice in Washington.

Currently, faith leaders from a plethora of traditions are intensely trying to add this essential addition to the Gun Violence agenda. To be sure, we also support the magazine cap, universal background

---

[43] From "A Prayer for Peace", Siddur Sim Shalom for Shabbat and Festivals, (RA/USCJ 1998), p. 149

checks and investment in mental health initiatives. But we want more people to acknowledge that the daily face of gun violence in American is a not a white child in Connecticut, but rather a minority child in New Orleans or Gary, Indiana.

We cannot turn a blind eye to the violence taking place in this country, whether it takes place in an inner city park or on Park Avenue.

In Parashat Yitro, God tells Moshe to say to the people:

> Now if you obey Me fully and keep My covenant, then out of all nations you will be My treasured possession.[44]

The Ishbitzer Rebbe teaches: do not read "treasured possession, instead read the words as "treasure chest."

By entering into a covenant with God, God implants within each of us the potential to bring goodness and blessing into the world. Thus we are not chosen because of who or what we are, but only because of what we contain. We contain the ability to help this country heal.

“Some may be guilty, but all are responsible,” wrote Abraham Joshua Heschel.

So true do his words ring today.

---

[44] Exodus 19:5

THE BLOOD OF THE CHILDREN CRIES OUT FROM THE GROUND![45]

Rabbi Gary S. Creditor

Over the many years that I can remember, beginning with the assassination of President John Kennedy with a rifle, the sound of the bullet was echoed by the citation of the second amendment and the "right to bear arms." Whenever a catastrophe occurs, whoever cites past catastrophes always omits the earliest ones, which never lose their terribleness, because it is too hard, too painful, too long a list to remember to recite all the names of all the places.

I want to talk about the "Right to Live." This is not the cliché lifted from the Declaration of Independence, "life, liberty and the pursuit of happiness," even as that is a very significant statement. I want to talk about the "Right to Live" of six and seven year olds to grow up, discover the universe, and fulfill their destinies. I want to talk about the "Right to Live" of the people dedicated to teaching them, who threw themselves in harm's way. I want to talk about the "Right to Live" of all innocent people, struggling in a difficult world, being good people, loving men and women, who are murdered, wantonly murdered by those with guns in their hands, in any place and at any time. Not just now.

I want to know something. Doesn't the "Right to Live" supersede the "right to bear arms?" Isn't there something more important than

[45] This sermon first appeared on Rabbi Creditor's blog (rabbigarycreditor.blogspot.com) on December 21, 2012.

guns? Isn't there something more fundamental than the caliber of the bullet? Isn't there something more precious than the rate of fire? Doesn't the "Right to Live" trump all other rights? To paraphrase the verse from Genesis from the story of Cain and Abel, "the blood of the children, the blood of their adult defenders screams out to Me from the ground." It is to them, the dead, to our children, the living, that the answers must be given.

I want to know something. Does the "right to kill" supersede the "Right to Live?" What is the purpose of guns? I remember being a little boy with a holster and cap guns. You had to put one cap in each and it made a bang. For some reason I had a Mattel gun that used a roll of caps and you could make a lot of sustained noise. I had no idea what I was doing. I had no idea what it meant. I don't know why my parents bought them for me. Our children never had toy guns. Never! Ever!

The blood of the children cries out from the ground: make us a better world! Make us a world of peace!

Stop the nonsense that guns don't kill! Yes they do! Yes, guns kill because they are held by people. Guns kill people. Guns kill animals. Killing begets killing, which begets more and more and more until there is no end! The blood of the children cries out from the ground: stop the killing! Who needs guns?!

I want to know something. Is the "Right to Live" held so cheaply because the profit is great from the proliferation of the "culture to kill" through video, movies, music – do you listen to the message of the lyrics? What is more important? To make money and elevate the culture of death? Or the culture of life? Is this the America we want? Is this the epitome of our society? Is this the "alabaster city?" Is this the country that we want God to bless?

I enjoy the old westerns on cable. Where is the blood? Where is senseless violence? None. Justice, honesty, truth were the elevated values that would triumph, but killing was not glorified. There was even a sense of remorse by the guy who was clearly good. Today it is reversed! The more gore, the more horror, the more blood and guts and cut open bodies, the more explosions and destructions. Just because there is the technical capability to show all this, do we have to? Should we? Must we? What world are we making? Do we promote fine arts? Do we esteem classical literature? Do we elevate excellent music? What do you expect to reap, when the seeds of destruction are so blatantly planted? The blood of the children cries out from the ground: make us a better world! Make us a world of peace!

I want to know something. Against whom are we bearing arms? Do we fear invasion from our neighbors to the north and south? Do we fear our neighbors who live next door? Do we intend to confront the local and state police? Would not intruders be more deterred by active alarm systems? Will the ability to defend against an intruder outweigh the number of deaths caused by people with guns who are ill-trained and ill-tempered? Will the proliferation of more guns, in a society already more armed than any in the world, make us safer, securer, surer? Are these quasi-military, high powered, quick-firing guns, the ones used to shoot duck, deer and antelope? The blood of the children cries out from the ground. They demand to know: who needs these guns?

How many tears must be shed by human beings? How much blood must spill in movie theatres, college campuses, high schools, elementary schools, shopping mall parking lots? How many hearts must break when the bell tolls as each name is read, as each tender body is buried?

I want to know something. I remember when living in New York it was decided to close facilities dealing with mental health, as it was deemed better to integrate these people into society at large. It never happened. If they had, they were abandoned to their families who did not have means to cope with the needs. Otherwise, they were on the streets. It really wasn't the philosophy, it was the cost. They would rather build prisons that honestly deal with the needs of society. They didn't want to deal with people. People with mental issues are "nobody's fault." They are members of our universal family. They are the easiest to cut in any budget. They are seemingly invisible. They don't have a lobby like the NRA. Now, now, it is on the agenda! The blood of the children cries out from the ground: this is the real cliff! This is the real cliff over which our world is destroyed! Fix it! Repair it! Mend it! Do not ignore us!

I want to know something. How many innocent deaths will it take for our elected officials to be leaders with moral backbones and not wimps who pander for votes? Where is their moral courage to face the mirror and know that day after day they have labored in society's vineyard to make each hamlet, each town, each county, each city better for each boy and girl, infant and adult, young and old, reach and poor, healthy and ill? How many tears must be shed by human beings? How much blood must spill in movie theatres, college campuses, high schools, elementary schools, shopping mall parking lots? How many hearts must break when the bell tolls as each name is read, as each tender body is buried? What must it take for delegates, senators, representatives, and president will finally act?

Until then, every morning, noon and night, at the break of dawn and the setting of the sun, in the dead of night and the brightness of the midday sun.

The blood of the children cries out from the ground! And it will continue to cry and cry, scream upon scream, like those in Newtown, Connecticut, until someone, *someone* will give them an answer.

The Blood of Your Fellow

Rabbi Daniel Kahane

"*Lo Ta'amod Al Dam Rei'echa* - do not stand idly by the blood of your fellow."[46]

This is a moral imperative that stands at the very basis of who we are. Yet, so far, despite this principle, we have not been able to garner enough outrage to change the law, to make sure these tragedies do not keep happening on a regular basis.

There is a saying in the Talmudic tractate of Sotah that people cannot commit a sin unless a "spirit of folly" enters them. What is the folly in this case, which has caused so many of us to stand idly? Are we not seeing the "Dam," the blood? Certainly in light of the coverage of the massacre that took place in Newtown this year that cannot be the case.

I humbly suggest that the problem is with the next word of this commandment, the "Rei'echa" aspect, the part about "your fellow."

The national conversation about gun control is all theory until it happens to someone you know. The reality is that I myself would not be writing this were it not for the fact that I found out today that my co-worker for seven years, someone I passed by the hall and said good morning every day, was shot (or shot herself, the details are still unclear). She is now in a comma, and even if she survives, she will have lost practically all vision, as well as most cognitive and motor skills.

---

[46] Leviticus 19:16

She is not only a co-worker, she is also the mother of a small child, who just a week ago came to the office and a hung a picture of a zebra he made for her, because she "liked black and white" and "was the best mommy ever." How will this boy spend this upcoming Mother's Day, and every other one for that matter, for the rest of his life?

Perhaps this question bothers me more than it bothers you, dear reader, simply because she is so clearly my "Rei'echa," my fellow. However, the reality is that she is your "Rei'echa," too. We have to remember that; we are all in this together, we are all One. We have to remember that, otherwise we are lost as human beings.

"*VeAhavta leRei'echa Kamocha, Zeh Klal Gadol BaTorah* - love your fellow as yourself[47], that is the great fundamental principle of the Torah."[48] These words were uttered by Rabbi Akiva, who loved so deeply and lost so much. If we cannot love our fellows as ourselves, let us at the very least recognize them as such, and not just stand idly by their blood.

---

47 Leviticus 19:18

48 Sifra, *Kedoshim*, 4

GUNS AND MOSES

Rabbi Joshua Hammerman[49]

The Ten Commandments include that oft-misinterpreted, "Thou shalt not kill."[50] The Hebrew word found there is not "kill," but "murder." Judaism does allow some killing, including the killing of animals for food – albeit in a strictly regulated, humane fashion – and the killing of human beings in self-defense, including morally justifiable wars.

But murder is a different matter entirely. The prohibition includes traditional concepts of cold-blooded criminal behavior, but the commentator Ibn Ezra explains that the definition of murder goes beyond that. He writes:

> One may murder by the hand and by the tongue, by tale bearing and character assassination. One may murder also by carelessness, by indifference, by the failure to save human life when it is in your power to do so.

By this understanding, 30,000 Americans are murdered by guns every year. In addition, there are hundreds of thousands of walking wounded in the United States, people like Gabby Giffords whose lives have been unalterably changed by those hand-held weapons of mass destruction that we call guns. The Torah has commanded us not to be indifferent in this matter. And now, in the aftermath of a string of unbearable tragedies, culminating in Newtown, the call for common sense gun reform has become the moral cry of this generation.

---

[49] A version of this essay appeared on Rabbi Hammerman's blog (joshuahammerman.blogspot.com) on January 31, 2013.
[50] Exodus 20:13

That's why, when extended a special invitation, I went to Washington recently, to join 80 clergy organized by Lifelines to Healing. We received a White House briefing from the Vice President's senior staffers working on this issue and then we presented our joint clergy statement, "Healing the Soul of America from Gun Violence," both to the Administration and then to a press conference on Capitol Hill. As we ascended the Hill, it became clearer than ever before why I was there. Like Abraham Joshua Heschel with Martin Luther King in Selma so many years before, I felt like we were "praying with our feet."

This is nothing less than the Civil Rights movement of our time. This is a true "Right to Life" initiative, in fact, one that cuts across all lines of race, socioeconomic background and creed.

Let the lost children of Gun Violence now become the fourth child at our Seders this year, along with the Newtown 20 and all the children, everywhere, who have fallen victim to our society's gun-sanity: they are the "child who cannot ask," because we allowed them to be killed on our watch.

As our statement says:

> We affirm that every life is precious in the eyes of our creator and our God has no pleasure in the death of anyone. We are committed to uniting around the common pain and loss of those who have suffered in Newtown and New Orleans, Chicago and Columbine and Oak Creek and Oakland. We are committed through our work to heal the soul of a nation. We will be vigilant partners in the struggle to transform our communities from the valley of the shadow of death to the land of the living.

Ridding our schools, streets and homes of gun violence is a moral issue of the highest order. People think that current attitudes will never change, but they are changing as we speak, just as they changed over the past generation regarding smoking, seat belts and littering. Gun owners and NRA members understand the need for common sense reform, especially regarding background checks. Nearly 90 percent of Americans support this.

No doubt, guns have become an enormous part of American culture, so much so that even at a conference devoted to reducing their impact, we kept on finding ourselves using expressions like "armed with arguments," "shoot from the hip," and "fire away." (I'm purposely refraining from using "bullet points" in this article.)

Gun violence is about teen gangs and angry husbands, it's about homicide and suicide, it's about household accidents with make-believe cowboys and it's about mentally unstable (and undiagnosed or unreported) young adults armed to the teeth. Until Aurora and Newtown, most in suburbia paid little heed to the massacres occurring every day in America's inner cities. As one red state evangelical minister stated plainly at my conference, "Shame on us."

> **We are guilty of betraying the Sixth Commandment because of our misguided understanding of the Second Amendment.**

Now we are feeling their pain too – for just as God feels the pain of all children equally, so should we weep not only for those innocent victims in Newtown, but for 15 year old Hadiya Pendelton, who was shot a mile from the President's Chicago residence this week, after seeing him sworn in last week as a majorette in her school band. And we weep with Shirley Chambers the Chicago mother who lost all four of her children to gun violence. All human life is of equal value. Let those four Chambers children now become the fourth child at our Seders this year, along with the Newtown 20 and all the children, everywhere, who have fallen victim to our society's gun-sanity: they are the "child who cannot ask," because we allowed them to be killed on our watch.

Yes, Ibn Ezra was right. "Thou Shalt Not Murder" means all of us, all who have allowed human beings to be murdered when we could have done something to stop it. We are guilty of betraying the Sixth Commandment because of our misguided understanding of the Second Amendment.

In fact, the Second Amendment is not in any danger of being violated if we take semi-automatic assault weapons, the ones designed for military use, out of the hands of civilians. No one is violating any sacrosanct freedoms if we ban high capacity magazines, like the one used in Aurora. No, in fact, we are defending a sacred freedom: the freedom to stay alive. And let's face it: *the NRA is funded 80 percent by gun manufacturers.* For their leadership, this isn't about defending freedoms. This is about defending profits.

In Detroit recently, a third grader came to school with a gun. A third grader! When the police asked why, he said, "I need it for protection."

Guns or People?

The old argument that guns don't kill people, people do, no longer holds up (if it ever did). Wayne LaPierre's claim that the only thing that stops a bad guy with a gun is a good guy with a gun is fatally flawed. Our sources tell us that the world is not full of bad and good people. We are all good and we are all bad. Moses himself was bad at times – he killed an Egyptian officer, after all, when his own life was not in danger. What drove him was anger, and anger got the better of him much later on, as well, when he disobeyed God's command by hitting the rock rather than speaking to it.[51]

It was for that incident that Moses was denied entry into the Promised Land. Some might think it a harsh punishment, but the Torah offers a clear message that excessive violence can never be tolerated. Moses was angry at the people, calling them rebels, and his anger got the best of him. He resorted to blows rather than words.

If even Moses, our greatest leader, was susceptible to irrational violence, then it's not about crazy people doing crazy things; it's about perfectly normal and good people who fly off the handle and do crazy things. The difference is, now we have semi-automatic rifles, the kind built by Russians to kill Nazis, and these rifles are designed to spray bullets without carefully aiming, to hit soldiers randomly. Those are the bullets that hit Shirley Chambers' 15 year old daughter randomly, and so many more.

---

[51] Numbers 20:12

Back in Moses' time, people got just as angry as they do now, but it was much harder to kill. And people did not take such pride in their weaponry. It's hard to imagine that Moses (the original Moses, not the guy who played him) would have said that his trusty rod would have to be pried from "my cold, dead hands." Given his history, if he had wanted to trade his rod in for a rifle, Moses might have had to wait a bit before passing a background check.

I would venture to guess that while people in our time get no angrier, they do get a lot more depressed. Mental illness effects one in four. Suicide rates are rising, especially among young people and the military, and suicide is much more likely to be "successful" when you stick a gun in your mouth than when you overdose on pills. When you use a gun, there usually is no second chance.

The Torah understood how serious violence can become when it spirals out of control.

The Torah understood how serious violence can become when it spirals out of control. The spinning bullet is the embodiment of that spiral. And like a diamond, a bullet is forever. Anger and depression impact us all. That does not make us bad people. Pills and rods don't necessarily kill. Sticks and stones merely break bones. But a gun in the hand of an angry man or depressed woman – it's the gun that kills, Mr. LaPierre.

It's the gun that kills.

Rebuilding an Alliance and Saving Jews

Assault rifles and large magazines must be banned. Even if it looks like Congress won't muster the votes, remember that Martin Luther King came to Washington and told President Johnson it was time for a voting rights act. Johnson said he had already spent his political capital and that it would take ten years. The Civil Rights Act was a reality within ten months.

I am proud that I was joined by 8 other rabbis among the 80 at the conference. Given that a major focus of these conversations was the plight of the inner city, this gave us a chance to begin to rebuild that alliance between African Americans and Jews that was so strong in the '60s. This possibility was not lost on us. We were touched by their pain and they appreciated our mere presence. And we also understood that this is an issue that is paramount for all of us. It just took Newtown to wake us up to that fact.

Before Newtown there was Northridge – the JCC shooting in 1999. As a Jew, I care about all innocent human beings, but I also know that my own people are especially threatened by a gun running culture that allows, through gun show loopholes, for white supremacists like Buford Furrow Jr. to procure unconscionably lethal weapons without a problem and blast 70 gunshots into the complex with the intent of killing lots of Jewish kids.

Ending this plague is a moral imperative AND a Jewish imperative. It is universal and particularistic. It is the cry of our generation.

Ending this plague is a moral imperative AND a Jewish imperative. It is universal and particularistic. It is the cry of our generation.

That's why I won't let my Congressional representatives off the hook. The President's Plan to Protect Our Children and Our Communities by Preventing Gun Violence is robust enough to address all major aspects of this crisis, including school security and mental illness. But it must be passed in full.

Life has become cheap indeed in America, a country where someone was likely killed by gun in the time it took for me to write this essay. 30,000 per year is 30,000 too many.

For our children's sake, this gun-sanity must stop.

FOR THEIR SHOES

Rabbi Menachem Creditor

For their shoes, Adonai.
For their damn shoes.
Shoes, Adonai!

Three children were shot for their shoes.
Their shoes, Adonai!

Is this Your world?
The world You envisioned?
Where people shoot each other
for shoes?!

It's not that we won't hurt each other with
hands, sticks, rocks, cars, words...
But guns in the hands
of those who would
shoot someone over
shoes...

Adonai, it's too late for us to say
You should have done better.
But You should have.

Now it's our turn.
Now is the time.

shoes......

WAKING UP: GUN VIOLENCE & INEQUALITY[52]

Rabbi Lauren Grabelle Herrmann

"Awake, O you sleepers, awake from your sleep!
O you slumberers, awake from your slumber!
Search your deeds and turn in Repentance....
Look to your souls and better your ways and actions."[53]

Moses Maimonides, the great medieval Jewish commentator, wrote these words about the **SHOFAR,** reflecting on the power and potency of this humble hollow instrument.

According to Maimonides, it is as if the Shofar cries to us:

> *Yo!* Stop sleeping! Wake up! Today, on Yom HaDin – The Day of Judgment - it's time to face some difficult truths! It's time to awaken to what we may be consciously or unconsciously ignoring! Examine our own actions and inactions! It's time for us to change our path so that we are better serving God, serving Truth!

This Rosh HaShanah, as the shofar is sounded, I am aware of hard truths I am awakening to. For through the very process of preparing for the High Holidays, I have found myself in the midst a "wake-up call," shaking me out of my complacency and calling me into action. Today, I share that wake-up call with you.

My journey toward waking up began on July 21, 2012.

---

52 This sermon was delivered at Kol Tzedek Synagogue in West Philadelphia on Rosh haShannah 5773/2012.
53 Maimonides, *Mishneh Torah, Hilchot Teshuvah* 3:4

I was staying with the kids at my mom's house the evening before. When I woke up the next morning, my mother told me about the shooting at the midnight showing of The Dark Knight in Colorado. Jon, my husband, a fan of the recent Batman movies, had been planning to go to a midnight showing that opening night. I breathed a sigh of relief – he didn't go! He was safe!

Though there were no incidents in any Philadelphia movie theatre– the thought of a mass shooting 1,700 miles away from us was enough to shake me into the recognition that I could lose him in a split second. The randomness of the violence, the idea of innocent people doing the most American thing possible – watching a Hollywood Blockbuster – just all seemed so crazy and unbelievable. I joined with much of the nation in the shock of this tragedy.

The fact that these incidents occurred so close in time, compounded by the complete silence of either presidential candidate on the issue of gun control, propelled my desire to address the growing violence in my talks on the High Holidays.

And then, the summer continued and the shootings continued. A terrible assault motivated by hate and ignorance left six members of a Sikh religious community in Wisconsin dead. Then, on August 24, a disgruntled former employee fired a gun in the middle of Manhattan, shooting eight people and killing one. Three days later, a Baltimore, Maryland boy opened fire on the first day of school.

The fact that these incidents occurred so close in time, compounded by the complete silence of either presidential candidate on the issue of gun control, propelled my desire to address the growing violence in my talks on the High Holidays.

My initial focus turned to the proliferation of guns in our country, the easy access of guns and of course, the illegal sale of guns that enables those with criminal backgrounds, mental illness, or who are underage to acquire firearms. In that process, I learned some harrowing statistics. There are nearly 90 guns for every 100 people in this country.[54] More than 30 people are shot and murdered each day, half of them are between the ages of 18 and 35. In Philadelphia, on the average, at least one person has been murdered every day over the last 25 years — and more than three-quarters of them have been killed with a gun.[55]

But in my search, something happened - something moved me, challenged me, changed me. I learned about and began to understand *the interconnection of gun violence and inequality.* The way in which these two toxic aspects of our society (easy access of guns and vast economic and racial inequalities) co-mingle, creating a society that ignores, devalues, and abandons poor and minority communities.

> **"What links America's high concentration of guns and relatively high level of gun deaths are the country's high levels of inequality, segregation and poverty."**
> **-Gary Younger**

One article, a commentary by Gary Younger in *The Nation*, written in the aftermath of the Aurora shootings, was particularly enlightening and instructive. Younger critiques the culture of "shock" in relationship to gun violence in America, saying that while violence like the massacre in Aurora is abhorrent, it is not at all shocking or random. Violence and death due to guns is part of the fabric of our country - it happens all the time, every day, it's just that we don't necessarily hear about it.

Younger notes that the night after the Aurora shooting, twenty two people were shot, three fatally, in Chicago. The Philadelphia organization GunCrisis, which through photos and journalism, brings to light the seemingly ceaseless violence in our city, noted that in the *four weeks* after Aurora, there were more than 115 victims of gun violence in Philadelphia- and there were more than 140 shootings in the City of Brotherly Love in the month of August alone.

Younger debunks the notion that guns and gun access is the only

---

[54] Gary Younger, "With Aurora, Another Mass Killing Shocks America. Why?" *The Nation*, July 25, 2012.
[55] Guncrisis.org

thing responsible for the violence of our society. He points out there are other countries with a high number of gun ownership -countries like Sweden, Finland, and Switzerland- that do not have a high number of gun murders. Younger writes, "What links America's high concentration of guns and relatively high level of gun deaths are the country's high levels of inequality, segregation and poverty."

In his article, Younger says words that sting with painful truth:

> There are places in America where you are supposed to be safe—shopping malls, suburban schools, cinemas – and there are places where people are expected to be vulnerable: poor black and Latino neighborhoods. The possibility of arbitrary death...is just understood as the price you pay for being black or Latino in America.

The experience of reading this and really taking it in – was like having a loud, piercing *tekiah gedola*, a long, piercing blast from the shofar, sounded right in my ear.

How could I so easily tune out and keep segmented the realities that are so close to me – literally, just a few blocks away from where I live, shop, walk, pray?

Here I was in disbelief about a movie theatre shooting—which of course was terrible and heinous —but I didn't know about those crimes that happened in my own city, not to mention other cities, in the days and weeks following. One of the reasons I decided to live and raise a family in the city is so that I specifically wouldn't be sheltered from these truths.

How could I so easily tune out and keep segmented the realities that are so close to me – literally, just a few blocks away from where I live, shop, walk, pray?

Admittedly, the reality of violence and its pervasiveness in our city and the country is not "new information." I do live in Philadelphia after all, among the most violent cities in the country. I had direct exposure to some of what goes on every day through pastoral work at The Hospital of University of Pennsylvania after graduation from rabbinical school. During the monthly overnight visits, I saw teenagers coming in with bullet wounds. I was there with families who were arrived to learn that their son or brother or father had been shot and was going into emergency surgery which may or may not save them. And since then, from the safety of my own home on 45th Street, I have heard noises coming from a close distance, and hoped upon hope that they were fireworks or a car backfiring but knowing that was likely not the case.

Yet, there is a difference between "knowing" – with my mind – and "knowing" with my heart and soul. It is the difference between on the one hand, having some nebulous understanding of a national problem and on the other hand, being present with the magnitude of what's happening day to day, being affected by the stories and by the tragedy of it all.

There is a difference between "knowing" – with my mind -- and "knowing" with my heart and soul.

It is letting my heart open to the pain of sons and daughters lost, of hope lost.

I want to share a story I heard over the last few weeks which was particular affecting. Marla Davis Bellamy, director of CeaseFire PA, tells a story that speaks to the brokenness of a society in which violence is normalized.[56] She describes the scene a case worker witnessed while hanging signs on a street in North Philly. It was a nice summer day, people were sitting on stoops and about 100 kids were playing on the playground. Suddenly, a young man took out a gun and opened fire. All the kids ducked. When the shooting stopped, the kids simply got up and started playing again—*like nothing had happened at all.* Not a single parent or guardian came out to take their child inside, not a single child ran home to take comfort or protection from an elder. No person reacted as if this was anything out of the ordinary. Can we imagine if such a thing happened at Clark Park?

Another story that touched me deeply was the story of Kianna Burns, a teenager who spoke in an interview on Radio Times about witnessing her father's murder (which happened as he intervened to break up a fight involving her brother) and who herself was shot in

---

[56] Interview on Radio Times, August 24, 2012

the leg trying to escape the incident. Despite the gruesome details of the story—of which I will spare you - what hit home most was her sharing how she is afraid to leave her house because of the violence that surrounds her. She travels to and from school, still hoping to graduate, but other than that—she stays at home as much as possible. It is near impossible for me to imagine that a young person - who should be hanging out with her friends and doing what teenagers do - feels that she can only "make it out alive" is if she stays inside as much as possible.

Coming to a new understanding and opening my heart to these and other stories... I have woken up. *And I am angry.* I am angry that I live in a country in which people are dying every day, kids fear for their lives, and safety is elusive. I am ashamed and upset that I, an educated, progressive person who cares about inequality, can live in such blissful ignorance of my own privilege, that I can so easily ignore this problem. I am deeply pained that we live in a society where poverty is a predictor of not only your future success but of your future survival.

I have woken up. *And I am angry.* I am angry that I live in a country in which people are dying every day, kids fear for their lives, and safety is elusive.

And at the risk of being *chutzpadik*, I think that all of us should also be angry and pained and saddened by what goes on just a few blocks from where we are sitting and all over our city and our country. We should be angry that teenagers use guns because they feel they have no other way. We should be disturbed by the fact that our media mourns shootings deemed "out of the ordinary" but doesn't take special note of the day after day murders that happen in poor and primarily African-American neighborhoods.

We should be saddened by the fact that children are "accustomed" to the sounds of gunshots and the rituals of funerals. In the words of Martin Luther King Jr.,

> Let us be dissatisfied until the tragic walls that separate the outer city of wealth and comfort and the inner city of poverty and despair shall be crushed by the battering rams of the forces of justice. Let us be

> dissatisfied until those that live on the outskirts of hope are brought into the metropolis of daily security.[57]

But this is not where the wake-up call ends. This is where the call begins. Being angry or frustrated or pained or dissatisfied *can* be a good thing – but only if it spurs us into action, only if we choose to take those raw emotions and channel it for something that is better.

This is, in fact, what Maimonides teaches us about the shofar. He says that the piercing blast of the shofar call to us, beckoning:

> Awake, O you sleepers, awake from your sleep! O you slumberers, awake from your slumber! Search your deeds and turn in Teshuvah, in Repentance....Look to your souls and better your ways and actions.

The call of the shofar is actually twofold: the first call is to wake up: the second call is to turn our wakefulness into action.

The call of the shofar is actually twofold: the first call is to wake up: the second call is to turn our wakefulness into action. We are to look to our souls, to discern what it is that we can do, and to better our ways and actions.

In the spirit of this teaching and in the hopes that we *can* turn and better our actions, I want to offer some direction for how we might stay awake and engaged in the coming year and beyond.

It may sound simple, but *in order to stay awake, we need to know what is going on in our city.* If we do not educate ourselves and stay informed, it will be easy for the violence in our city to fade again into the distance.

Through this process of discernment and education, I learned about an invaluable resource for keeping me informed. GunCrisis.org, through photos and daily updates and analysis, documents the crisis of gun violence in Philadelphia, filling in the gaps in the media's

---

[57] Martin Luther King, "Where do we go from here," Speech to Southern Christian Leadership Conference, August 16, 1967

coverage of the problem. Using awareness as a tool, we can speak out and challenge the culture of our media which deems some events "tragic" while others not even "newsworthy". We can let our voices be heard against both the proliferation of guns (especially illegal guns) in our society and about the interconnection of gun violence and inequality. When an incident happens around the country, we can name the truth that gun violence is not a "random event" but a crisis that threatens the lives of our young people and diminishes our future.

Being aware of the problem is an important step; being aware of solutions even more vital. It behooves us to know about and to support people and organizations that are making a difference.

Being aware of the problem is an important step; being aware of solutions even more vital. It behooves us to know about and to support people and organizations that are making a difference.

Through this process, I have learned about organizations like CeaseFirePA, which aims to stem the tide of gun violence in Philly's 22cd district, the most violent in the city, and to raise awareness of this issue on the city and state level.

A month ago, I didn't even know about this organization; now, I pledge my financial support and also plan to participate in the advocacy work they lead. Supporting those who are doing work in the field to seek peace and change communities is integral way we can stay awake and engaged on the issue. As our tradition teaches, giving *tzedakah* is not an act of "charity" – it is using our resources to balance out the scales, to move us toward more Justice (*Tzedek*) and equality.

Perhaps most importantly, we can also join with others to address the problems in our neighborhoods and communities, such as *Heeding God's Call*, a Philadelphia organization made up of churches, synagogues, and mosques, whose mission is "to inspire hope, raise voices, and take action to end gun violence."[58] After a spike in violence or a particular incident, members of *Heeding God's Call* will go out to the spot in which the homicide took place and literally stand witness, in order to both humanize the losses that happen day after day and to draw media attention to these underreported crimes.

I anticipate what some of you may be thinking: "*Rabbi, even these actions will not truly alleviate the crisis in our city and our nation. This problem is too complicated, too entrenched for us to really make an impact.*" I understand this concern. And I do feel that fatigue that comes when looking at problems that seem beyond what I can do.

But, in the face of the enormity and intractability of injustice and inequality, I take comfort and inspiration from the words of Abraham Joshua Heschel, of blessed memory, who said:

> Daily we should take account and ask: What have I done today to alleviate the anguish, to mitigate the evil, to prevent humiliation? Our concern must be expressed not symbolically, but literally; not only publicly, but also privately; not only occasionally, but regularly. What we need is the involvement of every one of us as individuals.

As Heschel points out: it is not the task of someone else "over there" to change what needs to be change: it is our task. To remember that it is not someone else's responsibility to care for our neighbor: it is our responsibility. To recognize that while we cannot necessarily complete the task, we are not free to abandon it.[59]

This year, when we hear the piercing blasts of the shofar:

Let us awaken out of our sleep! May we be able to fully listen, to be present with what is difficult and challenging in our city and in our world so that we can be true and faithful witnesses.

Let us look at our souls and turn in Teshuvah! Let us look inside and consider what each one of us can do to better our neighborhood, our city, our world. Let us turn toward the problem and not away from it.

---

[58] heedinggodscall.org

[59] Pirke Avot 2:21

Let us examine our deeds and better our ways! Let the shofar blast be a clarion call to action. May those actions, no matter how seemingly small, inspire us, our neighbors, and our community.

May this be a year of blessing, of equality, justice, and peace for all who dwell on earth.

RISING TO FACE INDIFFERENCE TO GUN VIOLENCE

Rabbi David Baum

I recently asked my congregants to raise their hands if they have been directly affected by gun violence. In a room of close to one hundred people, less than ten people raised their hands.

On January 28, 2013, I was one of nine rabbis from various movements who was invited as part of a group of around eighty faith leaders from all religions and denominations organized by PICO[60] Lifelines to Healing, a group that organizes faith leaders around various issues that impact faith communities, to travel to Washington, D.C. to discuss the issue of gun violence with each other, White House, and Congressional leaders. I went because I was moved by the tragedy at Sandy Hook Elementary, the faces of those children, the story of Noah Posner. However, it was not just this incident that moved me and affected the Jewish community: the 1999 attack at the North Valley Jewish Community Center in Los Angeles, California, that injured five, including three little boys, and killed one person; and the perpetrator, a white supremacist with a history of mental illness, used a semi-automatic weapon spraying the room with 70 bullets. The shooting of Gabrielle Giffords, who identifies as a Jew, in Tucson, Arizona. Jews are just as susceptible to suicide as other populations, and over half of suicides among males, who represent 79% of all

[60] People Improving Communities through Organizing

suicides, are by firearm.[61] In Judaism, we don't view the overwhelming majority of suicides as a weakness, but as a result of disease, depression, or mental illness. Gun violence does affect the Jewish community, but I will be honest, watching the funerals and hearing those eulogies, hearing the stories of the affected families, and seeing the faces of those parents in Newtown, moved me more than before, just as it has moved this entire country.

I traveled to Washington D.C. to stand with my brothers and sisters from the faith community to give our perspective on gun violence and to make sure that this issue will still be on the forefronts of the minds of our nation's leaders. The conference room was filled with religious leaders from many different backgrounds and faiths, but the majority were African-American pastors. We had a great time together, talking about our lives as religious leaders in this country, getting to know each other in our short time together, but it was not all fun and games.

At one point, we were asked to write down our own personal stories of gun violence. Here was the problem: few rabbis had direct stories, but the pastors sitting at our tables did. Pastor Michael McBride, the director of the Lifelines to Healing campaign and pastor of The Way Christian Center in West Berkley, told us this story: "Two years ago, I presided over the funeral of Larry, a teen from my congregation who was shot and killed in the Bay Area. More than 500 grief-stricken teenagers filled the pews that day, and I asked how many of them had been to more than one funeral. Far too many hands went up. I kept counting. Three funerals? Four? I got as high as ten, and more than half of the young people in the church wept as their hands remained lifted in the air."

I looked at the African-American pastors sitting at my table and they told me how many young people they bury due to gun violence. Burying three teens in a week, or a mother killed in a drive by shooting because they were on the street at night was not out of the ordinary. During one of our sessions, a pastor told us he had just received a text message: one of his eleven-year-old congregants, a little girl, was just shot in the face. A rabbi sitting at our table, Gary Creditor, told me a truly tragic story. He had converted an African-

---

61 "Suicide: At A Glance." *Centers for Disease Control and Prevention*. Centers for Disease Control and Prevention, 17 Oct. 2012. Web. 24 Apr. 2013.

American woman, a registered nurse, and her husband who then joined his community. This woman's son was killed in a drive-by shooting and she visited his grave everyday on her way to work at the hospital. One day, after visiting her son's grave and on her way to work, she too was killed during a drive by shooting, and Rabbi Creditor officiated at her funeral. The story he told me, with tears in his eyes, broke my heart. There are a multitude of similar stories: the story of the woman who lost all four of her children to gun violence, and that of 15-year-old Hadiya Pendleton who performed at President Barak Obama's second inauguration and a week later was shot in the back and died in Chicago. The pastors continued on, telling me about the fear that their congregants live through just walking in their neighborhoods, mothers kissing their children goodbye in the morning, wondering if their precious gifts will return.

I realized that I could somewhat empathize with them, and some of the rabbis at my table could also because many of us lived in Israel during the Second Intifada (2000-2005). I came to Israel to study just weeks after the bombing at the Frank Sinatra cafeteria where Jewish American students were murdered. Living in Israel during that time was not easy. I remember the feeling I had riding buses the few times I rode them, or the feeling of even walking by a bus, or of walking into a coffee shop or supermarket after being frisked by a security officer. Going to the *shuk* (open air market) on Friday afternoon, a joyful and exciting pastime became a time of looking over my shoulder in terror and fear. I felt what *B'nai Israel* (the children of Israel) felt as they were being oppressed in Egypt so many years ago, a *kotzer ruach* a crushed spirit (Exodus 6:9). Rashi, the famous medieval commentator (1040 – 1105), writes that the *kotzer ruach* is whenever "someone is under stress, his wind and his breath are short, and he cannot take a deep breath."

My heart would literally race as I walked through the streets of Jerusalem, and there were times when I felt I could not breathe. I remembered sitting at *minyan* (daily morning prayer) saying *tehillim* (Psalms) for the five, ten, fifteen or twenty Israelis who were killed in a suicide bombing the previous day, or even one time hearing a bombing in the morning, waiting for sirens, and saying *tehillim* (Psalms) because we assumed the worst. I was lucky, and so was Israel. In time, after certain measures, the bombings stopped, but for my brother and sister pastors in the inner cities of our country, the feeling of a crushed spirit, the *kotzer ruach*, of living in terror continues day after day.

Pastor Michael McBride told us, "Sandy Hook was a tragedy beyond belief, but Sandy Hook, the killing of kids at the hands of a gunmen, happens every day in our neighborhoods." The pastors, people of God, are frustrated. They are frustrated because the tragedy of children dying has been happening for years unabated. In their words, we Americans might mourn for a white child and a black child differently, but God loves them all the same. Perhaps we should open our eyes, to see what is literally within. The Talmud writes that there are three instances when a Jew cannot defend his or her life, and one of those cases is when someone asks you to kill someone else lest you be killed. As the Rabbis said, "Is my blood redder than his?" Our children may live in different neighborhoods, they may dress differently, they may have different color skin, but the blood is always the same color.

The first Shabbat I returned to my synagogue after this gathering was *Parashat*[62] *Yitro* [Exodus 18:1 – 20:22] which includes the famous Ten Commandments. There is a custom in synagogues during the recitation of the Ten Commandments where congregants rise to their feet, as if our rabbis were ordering us to honor these words and take them to heart. The first five contain lengthy explanations, but commandments six, seven, eight, and nine, are very brief and read in quick succession. Interestingly enough, these last four commandments do not need much explanation: *Lo Tirtzach*, you shall not murder; *Lo Tinaf*, you shall not commit adultery; *Lo Tignov*, you shall not steal. You shall not murder seems to make sense, but one word can make a big difference. It does not say *Lo Taharog*, do not kill; rather it states, do not murder. Thinking about this term, "murder," takes me back to Genesis, to the story of Cain and Abel, when one brother spills the blood of another. Back then, there were no laws against murder. In a split second, Cain, out of frustration and jealousy, spills his brother's blood. "Cain said to his brother Abel…and when they were in the field, Cain set upon his brother Abel and killed him (literally, *V'Yhargehu*)" [Genesis 4:8]. I always wondered why the Torah does not use the word *retzach* (murder) in this case. My interpretation: God never told humanity that taking another's life was not allowed, perhaps God assumed it, and yet, the first instance of

[62] The section of one of a biblical book read on Shabbat every week.

death in the entire Bible comes not from the hands of God, but by the hands of a human. God was shocked that this happened, saying to Cain, "What have you done? Hark, your brother's blood cries out to Me from the ground!" [Genesis 4:10] The Hebrew does not say *dam* (blood), it uses the word, *damim*, (literally: bloods in plural), to which the Jewish Publication Society (JPS) commentary states that not only did Cain kill Abel, but all of his potential offspring are now doomed never to be born, as stated in Mishnah Sanhedrin 4:5, "Whoever takes a single life destroys thereby an entire world."[63]

Since creation, God had constantly tried to bring order to chaos, and He kept on failing. Once the world became too corrupt, he destroyed the world, and started over with Noah, but chaos overtook order again. The Egyptians oppressed a people and literally killed their little boys, drowning them in the Nile River. God sent plague after plague to the oppressors in Egypt, and one would think that the whole world would listen when the mighty Pharaoh was defeated, but right after liberation from oppression came Amalek who in our weakest moments, when we were tired, and hungry, killed those who were physically weak and lagged behind. As the JPS commentary states, "people whom anyone with elementary decency would avoid attacking!"[64] These very well could have been children! So how would God bring justice to the world, how would God bring order to chaos? God knew that it would have to come through Torah, a divine law imposed upon humanity. And finally the tide turned and order began to overtake chaos.

A just law, with its mate, morality, is stronger than any plague or any army.

A just law, with its mate, morality, is stronger than any plague or any army. I asked my grandfather, a survivor of the Holocaust from Czechoslovakia, would his family have been saved if they had an arsenal of weapons in their home? After all, weapons were

---

[63] Sarna, Nahum M. *Genesis/Bereshit : The Traditional Hebrew Text with New JPS Translation.* Philadelphia: Jewish Publication Society, 1989. Print. Genesis 4:10

[64] Tigay, Jeffrey H. *Deuteronomy/Devarim: The Traditional Hebrew Text with the New JPS Translation.* Philadelphia: Jewish Publication Society, 1996. Print. Deuteronomy 25:18

commonplace in his family. His father, my great grandfather Alexander Baum, was a high officer in the Czechoslovakian army and he had cousins who also served and were proficient in the use of weapons. But he told me something very interesting, "No amount of guns would have saved us. We would have been have saved had our neighbors not turned against us." During the Holocaust, Germany defeated the greatest armies in the Europe. France and Poland were considered the greatest military powers of the time, and when they were defeated, many of their citizens and leaders gave up their Jewish neighbors almost besting the Nazis with their virulent anti-Semitism. There were only three countries that did not give up any of her Jews: Bulgaria, Albania, and Denmark.[65] These countries were not known for their military might, but they showed their moral might by resisting the Nazis in this way. They could not sit idly by watching their neighbors taken to their deaths just because they were born Jews.

When God began to speak, and gave us His Torah, the notion of morality continued, and continues to this day. Let us return to the sixth commandment, *Lo Tirzach*, do not murder. The famous medieval commentator, Abraham Ibn Ezra (1089 – 1164) gives an interesting explanation and expands this commandment: "One may murder with the hand or with the tongue, by tale bearing or by character assassination. One may murder also by carelessness, by indifference, by the failure to save human life when it is in your power to do so."

> **"The opposite of good is not evil; it is indifference."**
> **– Elie Wiesel**

During one of the press conferences, an evangelical pastor stood up and told us about one of his favorite quotes told to him by Elie Wiesel. Mr. Wiesel told this pastor, "The opposite of good is not evil; it is indifference."

Listening to those holy words, I was reminded of the words of Rabbi Abraham Joshua Heschel who famously "prayed with his legs" on his march with Dr. Martin Luther King Jr. in Selma:

---

[65] *Besa: A Code of Honor. Muslim Albanians Who Rescued Jews During the Holocaust. Yad Vashem*. Web. 24 Apr. 2013.
http://www.yadvashem.org/yv/en/exhibitions/besa/introduction.asp

> "Morally speaking, there is no limit to the concern one must feel for the suffering of human beings, that indifference to evil is worse than evil itself, that in a free society, some are guilty, but all are responsible."[66]

How long will we stand by and hear the blood of our fellow citizens, men, women, and children, cry up from the ground? How long will military style weapons be in the hands of criminals and mentally ill? How long will we allow deadly weapons to be sold to anyone without a proper background check? How long will we hide our eyes and let chaos rule over order?

Now is the time to turn indifference into making a difference. Now is the time to stop the destruction of worlds by ensuring that our citizens, from Newtown to New Orleans, Chicago to Columbine, Oak Creek to Oakland, urban and suburban, of all faiths and colors, to live free from the terror of gun violence. Now is the time to act because all of us are responsible.

---

[66] Heschel, Abraham Joshua, and Susannah Heschel. *Moral Grandeur and Spiritual Audacity: Essays.* New York: Farrar, Straus and Giroux, 2001. Print.

GUN OWNERS: WHO WILL STAND UP AND SAY, 'ENOUGH?!'

Rabbi Aaron Alexander and Rabbi Ronit Tsadok

Shock. Disbelief. Outrage. Dismay. Brokenness. Anger. Sadness. Despair. These are just a few of the diverse emotions Americans have been feeling in the few weeks following our latest battle with the gun-violence epidemic. And rightfully so. The tragic loss of so many lives ought lead us to these very reactions.

But do we honestly still have the right to be surprised by these deadly attacks? Since 1989 there have been at least 40 incidents of school-related gun deaths in this country, which is not to mention the countless shootings in malls, movie theaters, houses of worship and homes. We continue to point fingers and attempt to find the one "reason" why this keeps happening. However, we can no longer intentionally ignore the fact that the sheer amount of guns in America contributes to our epidemic. In a recent New York Times piece we see that:

> Scientific studies have consistently found that places with more guns have more violent deaths, both homicides and suicides. Women and children are more likely to die if there's a gun in the house. The more guns in an area, the higher the local suicide rates. "Generally, if you live in a civilized society, more guns mean more death," said David Hemenway, director of the Harvard Injury Control Research Center. "There is no evidence that having more guns reduces crime. None at all." "More guns means more death." It

> is a statement that should not astonish us, yet in the weeks following the tragedy in Newtown, gun sales have significantly increased. This is cognitive dissonance at its most dangerous.[67]

The talmudic rabbis recognized long ago that inundating people who are susceptible to sin with the very tools that enable them to falter is almost inevitably going to lead to an undesired outcome. Just after asserting that the very nature of humanity is as hard-wired to misstep as it is to follow the straight-and-narrow, they praise Moses for his boldness in partly blaming God for the incident of the golden calf. The rabbis re-interpret a place name in the very first verse in Deuteronomy, *Di Zahav*. The plain meaning of the text, of course, is clear. *Di Zahav* is just another stop on the Israelite journey:

> These are the words which Moses spoke to all Israel beyond the Jordan; in the wilderness, in the Aravah, over against Suph, between Paran and Tophel, and Lavan, and Hatzerot, and Di-Zahav.[68]

But in this ambiguous name also lies a heteronymic opening to send a powerful message and reread the very same letters to mean *dai zahav*, or, "enough gold!"

> What is Di Zahav? The House of Yannai said - Thus is what Moses really said to God: "The silver and gold (*zahav*) that you showered upon the Israelites until they said enough (*dai*!) caused them to sin by making the Golden Calf.[69]

Which is to say, the Israelites themselves realized they were being inundated with huge quantities of Egyptian gold and would not be able to restrain themselves from reverting to idolatry. In the rabbinic imagination, Moses accuses God of setting the Israelites up for monotheistic failure by giving them the very tools with which they can, and ultimately do, make an idol. Should anyone, including God, be astounded by this cardinal sin? And when Moses realizes that God is going to punish the Israelites for this, he challenges divine will and calls God out on this unrealistic expectation.

They proceed to drive home this point with an unsavory parable:

---

[67] Elizabeth Rosenthal, *More Guns = More Killing*, New York Times, January 5, 2013
[68] Deuteronomy 1:1
[69] Babylonian Talmud, Berachot, 32a

> Rabbi Hiyya bar Abba said in the name of Rabbi Yohanan: Consider the case of a man who bathes, anoints, feeds and perfumes his son. And then he puts a purse of money around his son's neck and leaves him at the doorway of a brothel. Does anyone reasonably expect the son to avoid committing a sin?[70]

Seems pretty clear, right? The parable illustrates that even though each of us is imbued with the freedom to make choices, sometimes the circumstances are so "weighted" to a certain outcome that any expectation of the opposite is simply naive.

This is most certainly not an abdication of free will and accountability. Any such conclusion would invite a society unfathomable to the current American who is enmeshed in the value of liberty. But consider the gravity of this lesson. At a certain point the ability to *choose wisely* becomes overwhelmed by excess. Yes, the Israelites sinned, but - and here is Moses' boldness - God should not have encouraged them to keep acquiring, amassing and collecting. God should not have enabled their fears of scarcity and safety. They were humans, with a human weakness for using their freedom of choice in precarious ways.

Now is not the time to infuse our society with more guns. We have more than enough.

And that is precisely what this country suffers from right now. Three-hundred million guns. Fifty percent of the world's guns housed right here in America. Military style assault weapons easily purchased and hoarded. What do we honestly expect?

We have long tolerated the NRA's god-like power in our political system. Their successful lobbying has allowed for an influx of needlessly violent and scarily proficient weaponry into our fragile society. But now is not the time to infuse our society with more guns. We have more than enough. Too many of us are susceptible to misusing and/or abusing the abundance. What we need is a modern-

---

[70] Ibid.

day, courageous leader like Moses who will stand up and say, "Enough. Is. Enough!"

Gun-owning community: It has long been established that your Second Amendment *rights* will not be revoked. OK. But recognize that you are members of a community, and as part of that community you have a *responsibility* to find your inner Moses and courageously come forward to speak truth. This is beginning to happen in small ways. The message, though, needs to be viral. **Get your house in order**: 1) Get rid of the semi-automatic assault weapons. 2) Significantly increase the criteria required to purchase and own guns. 3) Don't allow for any possible loopholes in background checks. 4) Mandate, like many other civil societies, regularly scheduled safety training for all gun owners.

We now find ourselves in a liminal space, knowing that this is precisely the time in which we, together, will either effectively address our country's obsession with limitless and needlessly violent weaponry, or slide back into our typically self-focused and detached existence. Who will come forward and say "enough is enough!"?

IT IS TIME TO PUT A STOP TO THIS![71]

Rabbi Jack Riemer

There are certain churches that I know where the sermon that I am going to give today would get me into big trouble. I don't think that that is true of this synagogue--but if it is, then so be it.

I think that the time has come for America to put into practice a law of the Torah that is found in today's Torah reading. It is a law that I believe supersedes the Second Amendment to the Constitution—at least the way that that amendment is understood in certain circles.

This is the law:

> You shall not put a stumbling block before a blind person.[72]

The Sages of the Talmud looked at this verse and said: This cannot be what it means, for who would be so cruel as to purposely cause a blind person to trip and fall? Such a sadist would be so rare that it would not be necessary for the Torah to have a law forbidding him from doing such a thing. And therefore, they said, that this law must refer to a different kind of blindness, not just to the inability to see physically.

---

[71] This sermon is available, along with many others, through Rabbi Jack Riemer's *Torah Fax* (torahfax.com).

[72] Leviticus 19:14

The Sages of the Talmud came up with a number of examples of blindnesses to which this law would apply. For example, you are not allowed to offer a drink to a recovering alcoholic. If you do, you are tempting him and making it harder for him to stay on the wagon. A parent is not allowed to goad his adult son, for, if he does, he may drive his son into hitting him, which is something that is forbidden by the Torah.

There are a number of other examples of things that you are not allowed to do and that, if you do, you violate this law, but my favorite one is this:

> You are not allowed to sell a weapon to a man who is angry, for if you do, he may use it in his wrath, and you will be partially responsible for what he does.

This is the law that I believe it is time for our country to take seriously. For in recent years, we have had case after case after case of people who were either angry or who were mentally ill who have been able to obtain weapons and who have used these weapons to kill innocent people.

Let me give you just a few examples:

1. Phillip Markoff, a medical student, allegedly carried his semi-automatic in a hollowed-out volume of 'Gray's Anatomy". Police believe that he used it in a hotel room in Boston to murder Julissa Brisman, a young woman who had advertised her services as a masseuse on Craigslist.

2. In Palm Harbor, Florida, a twelve year old boy named Jacob Larson came across a gun in the family home that, according to what they told the police, his parents HAD FORGOTTEN they had. Jacob shot himself in the head, and is in a coma, police said. Authorities believe that the shooting was accidental.

3. When Phil Spector, the music producer, decided, for whatever reason, to kill the actress, Lana Clarkson, all he had to do was reach for his gun--one of the 283 MILLION PRIVATELY OWNED guns in this country!

4. When John Muhammad and his teenage accomplice, Lee Malvo, went on a killing spree that took the lives of ten innocent people in the Washington D.C. area, the least of their worries was how to obtain high-powered weapons with which to carry out their random killings.

5. Eleven years ago, the world learned the word 'Columbine' when two teenagers sprayed bullets into the bodies of their classmates before turning their guns upon themselves.

6. We all remember Columbine. The word has entered our language as a symbol of insane purposeless violence. But how many of us remember that just five months after Columbine, a man with a semi-automatic handgun opened fire on congregants praying in a church in Fort Worth, Texas? Eight people died that day, including the gunman, who shot himself.

7. A little more than a year before the massacre at Columbine, two teenagers with high-powered rifles killed a teacher and four little girls at a school in Jonesboro, Arkansas. If you don't remember this incident, I can't blame you. There have been so many such incidents at public schools in recent years that it is hard to keep track of them. Every new one that occurs pushes the previous one out of our memories.

8. Back in April, a man named Jiverly Wong, a refugee from Vietnam, stormed into a school for new Americans and killed thirteen people before killing himself. Eleven of his victims were new immigrants. They came from seven different countries--in Europe, Asia, and Africa. Some of them had fled violence in their own countries. All were attempting to build new lives here in America.

And the beat goes on. Three policemen in Pittsburgh were lured to their deaths by an assassin who killed them and then himself. On the campus of Virginia Tech a couple of years ago a student named Seung-Hu Cho entered a school building and slaughtered anyone and everyone he could find until he was cornered, and then he shot himself.

Why did they do it?

Since they are no longer available for analysis, we can only guess. But the fact that Wong sent a letter to the Binghamton newspaper and to the local television station with photographs of himself holding guns seems to indicate that he wanted attention and publicity. And the fact that Cho did the same thing seems to indicate that he, too, wanted his name, his face, and his grievances to be broadcast far and wide. And sure enough, their names, their faces, and their stories were broadcast. They got their fifteen minutes of fame, which is evidently what their sick minds craved.

Homicides are only a part of the story. While more than 12,000 people are murdered each year with guns, estimates are that more than 30,000 people are killed each year by guns. This includes the 17,000 who commit suicide each year with guns, and the 800 who are killed annually in accidental shootings, and the more than 300 each year that are killed by the police.

And then, there are the people who are wounded and who don't die. Nearly 70,000 fall into this category in a typical year, including the 48,000 who are criminally attacked, the 4,500 who survive suicide attempts, the more than 15,000 who are shot accidentally, and the more than 1,000 who are wounded by the police in shoot outs.

The medical cost of treating gunshot wounds in this country is estimated to be more than two billion dollars a year. Nonfatal gunshot wounds are the leading cause of uninsured hospital visits. The toll on children and teenagers is particularly high. According to the Brady Campaign, from which most of my statistics are drawn, more than 3,000 children are shot to death in an average year. More than 1,900 of these 3,000 are murdered, more than 800 are suicides, about 170 a year are killed accidentally, and twenty or so are killed by the police each year.

We are a culture soaked in blood. And the truth is that we have gotten used to it. We may tsk-tsk for a day or two after a particularly horrible incident, and we may say: 'someone ought to do something about this', but after that we go back to our lives and forget about it. We have become blasé about the amount of violence that drowns this country in blood every year.

We confiscate shampoo from carry-on luggage at airports while at the same time we hand out high-powered weaponry to criminals and psychotics at gun shows. And isn't that insane?

I know that there is a Second Amendment to the constitution that gives every person the right to bear arms. But was that amendment really meant to include the right to own machine guns? Was it really intended to protect the rights of the criminals and the mentally insane to buy arms? Was it meant to produce the blood baths that we are witnessing so often every year in our time? Does the National Rifle Association, which is one of the most powerful lobbies in Washington today, think that it is only protecting the rights of hunters and sportsmen to bear arms when it threatens anyone who wants to run for president or for congress in this country that, if they question the right to own guns, they will not be elected?

> **The statement in the Torah is clear. Now it is for us to hear it, and to understand it, and to act upon it.**

There may be some passages in the Torah that are outdated, that are no longer relevant in the world in which we live. But I can think of very few passages in all of ancient literature that are more relevant and that need to be taken seriously in our time as the verse that says: "Thou shalt not put a stumbling block before the blind". This verse, with the rabbinic elaboration that applies it to selling weapons to the weak minded, is more than just relevant. I believe that it is an urgent message to our blood soaked society.

Let me put it very bluntly:

The National Rifle Association is committed to keeping guns available to any and all those who want them--for whatever reason and in whatever mental state they may be. They are committed to keeping killing easy. And we should be just as committed to stopping them.

If there is anyone sitting here who is offended by what I have said today, then I am glad that I said it, for we have passed the point where we can sit quietly by and let the blood bath go on.

And if there is anyone sitting here today who agrees with what I have said, then I ask you to please join me in letting our leaders know that the NRA is not the only powerful lobby that they need to be afraid of. We need to let them know that we count too, and that we will judge them by whether they kow-tow to the NRA or whether they take a stand on behalf of the sacredness of human life, and against the wanton shedding of blood which stains the streets of our country.

The statement in the Torah is clear. Now it is for us to hear it, and to understand it, and to act upon it. If we do anything less than that, we will bear a measure of responsibility for the fact that our land is soaked in blood.

Several Questions

Rabbi Gary S. Creditor

I. Questions for the NRA:

I would like to ask the NRA just one question: "*What is your proposal to reduce gun violence in America?*" I could ask many questions, but this one is the most important. I don't need to search for statistics. I don't need to study the Second Amendment. I don't care who is a liberal and who is a strict constructionist.

This I do know: that every day I open my local newspaper, the Richmond Times-Dispatch - *every single day* - there is another report of violence with a gun. It seems that every single day of every single month throughout the whole year, that some place in the tri-cities area of Richmond, Virginia there is violence perpetrated with a gun.

My personal reading of the newspaper every single day tells me not to believe anyone who says that the rate of gun violence has diminished. No it has not! Cumulatively, either in robberies, woundings, murders, terrorizing, or other acts of criminality, guns are increasingly wreaking havoc in our society, endlessly, ceaselessly and with impunity.

Here is what the NRA does not want: The NRA does not want to infringe on anyone's right to have guns. The NRA does not want to infringe on anyone's rights to have guns that fire many rounds in very quick succession. The NRA does not want to infringe on anyone's rights to have magazines for guns that will enable them to fire many rounds in the minimum of time.

So I have a few questions for the NRA:

- What is your proposal to reduce gun violence in America?
- Do you really care?
- Is silence all we get?
- Is more guns all we get?

II. Questions for the Senators in the Congress of the United States:

- Do you read the daily paper?
- Do you pay attention to the articles on gun violence on the streets of every single city, town, hamlet and village in this country?
- Have you ever buried a person killed by a gun?" I have!
- Did you ever stare into their grave?" I have!
- If you were there, what were you thinking?
- Where you standing there calculating how many votes you would gain or lose?
- Where you considering your personal score with the NRA?
- Or did you just stop and think what this dead person could have done with their life instead of being in their grave?

I ask every single Senator, man or woman: What is more important to you – being re-elected or saving a life? And not just one life, many, many lives! *Do you care?*

III. Questions for everyone who reads these words:

- What have you done to help reduce gun violence in America?
- Have you signed petitions to the President, Senators and Representatives? If so, how many? How often? (And if you have, don't stop now!)
- Have you marched in the streets?

- Have you lain down on the ground as I did in Capitol Square as if I was dead?
- Imagine lying down, in silence on the cold ground looking at the sky through leafless branches, not moving and thinking that you are dead?
- Have you talked to your children about guns?
- Have you talked to your neighbor about guns?
- Or have you pulled on blinders and said: "Hear no evil; see no evil; know no evil"?

It is right outside our door! Gun violence is not a City of Richmond "problem." It is not an Henrico County "problem." It is not a Chesterfield, Hanover or Goochland Country "problem." It is everybody's problem. Every preacher from every pulpit can echo these words about their own locations.

Gun Violence knows no borders.
Gun Violence knows no age.
Gun Violence knows no gender.
Gun Violence knows no race, no ethnicity, no color.
Gun violence is an equal geographic, demographic monster.
Gun Violence kills Presidents, Senators, leaders, and the unknown.
Gun Violence destroys the rich and the poor.

Gun Violence is, in truth, the *Malach HaMavet,* the Angel of Death. But different from the Pesach ditty of Chad Gadya, **it is we**, not God, who must conquer the Angel of Death.

In the Book of Leviticus, 19:16, we read in the Hebrew: "Lo ta'a'mod al dam ray-eh-cha, Ani Adonai." The last two words simply mean "I, YHVH – translated as 'Lord/God.' In the verse its purpose is to given the ultimate imprimatur of our God upon the first half of the sentence. There are many attempts to translate it:

> "Do not profit by the blood of your fellow."
> "Do not stand aside the blood of your fellow."
> "Do not stand by the blood of your fellow.
> "Do not rise up against the life of your fellow."

I prefer the simple literal translation: **"Do not stand *ON* your neighbor's blood."** Whether we walk here or there, in public or in our backyard, in one part of the city or another, the very earth is stained, sullied, desecrated, violated by the blood shed anywhere. Are we capable of literally – not figuratively - standing ***on***, walking ***on*** the blood of others?

Who will answer my questions?

THE WEAPON'S SHAME: A CASE FOR GUN CONTROL IN JEWISH LAW[73]

Rabbi Ari Hart

Newtown, Aurora, Tucson, Littleton: hearing the names of these picturesque American cities once evoked images of the American dream. Now they evoke an American nightmare - mass gun violence. The wounds in Newtown are the freshest and probably the most horrific, but the scars of gun violence run deep throughout our country. Sometimes the media pays attention, bringing light to this horrific problem. Sometimes not: just last Friday afternoon and evening, hours after the Newtown shootings, at least 10 people in my hometown of Chicago were wounded by gunfire.

As we search for solutions in the aftermath, we turn to research, pundits and, for some of us, the wisdom of our faiths for guidance.

Jewish law, or *halacha* (the path), is a spiritual system that seeks to make our world a holier place by binding the loftiest values to the most practical realities. It offers guidance on every aspect of life, from working on prayer to paying workers, and everything in between. Though the majority of the *halachic* literature was composed before the invention of firearms, it contains several principles that can be directly applied to the current debates around

[73] This essay first appeared on Rabbi Hart's HuffPost blog on Dec. 18, 2012

guns.

The *Mishna*, a text of Jewish law codified in the second century C.E., frames the conversation powerfully. In a discussion of what clothes and jewelry may or may not be worn on the Sabbath, the Mishnah says the following:

> A man must not go out with a sword, bow, shield, lance, or spear [on the Sabbath]; and if he goes out, he must bring a sin-offering. Rabbi Eliezer said: They are ornaments for him. But the sages maintain they are merely shameful, for it is said, and they shall beat their swords into plowshares, and their spears into pruning hooks: Nation shall not lift sword up against nation, neither shall they learn war any more.[74]

What a powerful idea. Contrary to what the latest movie or video game tells us, weapons are not glamorous. They are reminders of fear, weakness and of our unredeemed world. In our culture, the gun is fetishized; its sexy, powerful portrayal unavoidable if one consumes any media: print, television, film, game, music. For the rabbis of the Mishna, it is ugly, shameful, not worthy of the holy Sabbath.

The weapon's shame does not render it forbidden though. Jewish law does affirm the right to defend oneself, to own weapons and even to sell weapons, so long as the purchaser is not a threat to others. Maimonides, the brilliant 12th century Jewish philosopher and legal scholar, ruled that one may not sell "knives, manacles, iron chains, bears, lions, or any object which can endanger the public"[75] to those who might cause the public harm.

The value of minimizing public harm is central to the Jewish case for gun control, though it is rooted in an unlikely source: stumbling blocks before the blind. Leviticus states, "*You shall not place a stumbling block before the blind.*"[76] This verse has been understood by generations of rabbis that one should not put unnecessary dangers or temptations in front of others.

---

[74] Babylonian Talmud, Shabbat 63a
[75] *Mishneh Torah*, Laws Pertaining to Murder, 12:12
[76] Leviticus 19:14

The medieval code of Jewish law, the Shulchan Aruch, writes:

> And for every stumbling block that threatens lives, one must remove it, protect oneself from it, and be exceedingly careful in its regard; as it says: "You shall guard and protect your lives," (Deuteronomy 4:9). And if the stumbling block is not removed and is placed in front of those who come to danger, one has violated a positive commandment.[77]

For someone filled with hatred or uncontrolled mental illness, what more dangerous stumbling block could there be then an automatic or semiautomatic weapon, like the Bushmaster .223 used in Friday's shooting?

We must be honest: better gun policies are not a complete solution and will not end killing. Many factors go into gun violence, including a media that glorifies guns, poor schools, broken families, inadequate mental health services and more. Put them all together, and we have a massive, deadly stumbling block for someone with evil in their heart or a disease in their head. But so long as we allow weapons designed to hunt human beings to be freely sold in our marketplace we amplify the potential damage these killers can do. We can change this. My faith issues the following call: "Do not stand idly by the blood of your neighbor."

How much more blood must be spilt before we stop standing by?

---

[77] Choshen Mishpat, 427:8

ARE THEY HIS ADORNMENTS? ON GUNS AND MASCULINITY[78]

Rabbi Aryeh Cohen

When I went to Israel in the mid-1970s to study in yeshivah for a year (which became two years, then five years, then *aliyah* and a life-long commitment, then twelve years), there was a moment ritualized in the surety of its repetition with every new cadre of American students.

As I was studying at a *hesder* yeshivah, all of my Israeli contemporaries were either serving or on the brink of serving in the Israeli army. As a result of this, our Israeli colleagues in the *bet midrash* and with whom we shared dorm rooms and lunch tables were — when on security detail — armed. This was quite a change from the urban and suburban lives that my American colleagues and I had led prior to our time at yeshivah. The reaction to this situation is fascinating in hindsight. The overwhelming response was awe. Here's the ritualized moment: At some time during the year, almost every one of the Americans would borrow one of the Israeli students' weapons (usually an M16 submachine gun), unloaded, and be photographed holding the gun. There were ancillary moments to this central ritual such as acquiring IDF shirts or hats or T-shirts.

[78] Reprinted with permission from *Sh'ma* (shma.com) November 2009 as part of a larger conversation on gun control.

However, all were secondary to the moment of posing with the weapon.

I feel the need to stress that these were seventeen-, eighteen-, or nineteen-year-olds who spent most of their waking hours studying Talmud. These were young men whose life experiences and cultural knowledge up until that moment had taught them to avoid people with weapons. Yet, here they were, venerating death-dealing weaponry. The weapons, of course, were not seen as *real*, as in "I might be in combat where I would have to fire a weapon at another person." They were props and the young men were Rambo or Ari ben Canaan for that moment.

While it would probably be seen as scandalous if the son of a Modern Orthodox family abandoned the professional track for a stint in the Marines, it would be seen as laudable if that same son joined the IDF paratroopers.

Holding the weapon was also a transitory cure for what might be called the diasporic malady — living historical powerlessness and oppression. These young men were exulting in the power of an army that was no more theirs than their powerlessness in North America; however, this momentary dream of masculinity served to assuage the learned powerlessness of the American Jewish community.

The contestation about the status of weaponry is inscribed in some of the earliest texts of Rabbinic Judaism — texts that were part of the core curriculum of these students. Mishnah Shabbat 6:4 records some regulations for what one may transport from a private domain to a public domain on Shabbat.

> A man may not go out with a sword or a bow or a shield or a club or a spear; and if he went out [with the like of these] he is liable to a sin-offering. R. Eliezer says: They are his adornments.
>
> But the Sages say: They are only a disgrace to him, for it is said (Isaiah 2:4): And they shall beat their swords into plowshares, and their spears into pruning-hooks, nation shall not lift up sword against nation, neither shall they learn war anymore.

Whether or not a man may carry his weapon from a private to a public domain depends on whether weapons are considered to be adornments like jewelry (*tachshitin*). If so, then it is parallel to what a woman is permitted to wear while going from a private to a public domain in this chapter of Mishnah. R. Eliezer claims that weapons adorn a man. They are intricately bound up with his masculinity and are a glory to it. As proof of his position, he draws support from a verse in Psalms (45:4): "*Gird your sword upon your thigh, O hero, in your splendor and glory.*" Rav Kahane, a Babylonian sage who made aliyah to the land of Israel, avers: "This verse refers to Torah study."

The American Jewish community is unsettled about what guns, army, power, and violence mean. While it would probably be seen as scandalous if the son of a Modern Orthodox family abandoned the professional track for a stint in the Marines, it would be seen as laudable if that same son joined the IDF paratroopers. Gun control is desirable in Los Angeles but guns are desired by Americans living in Jerusalem.

This should force us to face the question: Do we think that weapons adorn our communal masculinity?

Newtown and New Orleans, Oakland and Oak Creek

Rabbi Amy Eilberg – Post-PICO Meeting

I gratefully accepted Rabbi Menachem Creditor's invitation to attend a multi-faith meeting on gun violence, gathering clergy-activists from around the country in Washington, D.C. But I had no idea of how transformative the experience would be. Within minutes of sitting down at the table, I knew that I would leave this meeting changed.

These were not the usual suspects, at least in my experience. This was a group of approximately 80 clergy, the great majority of them African-American parish clergy from large American urban areas: Chicago, Detroit, Oakland, Sacramento, Cleveland, and New Orleans, drawn together by the Lifelines for Healing Program of the PICO Network ("People Improving Communities through Organizing," a faith-based organizing initiative in 150 American cities). Whites were a conspicuous minority -- 9 rabbis, a handful of white Protestant ministers, and one Catholic sister.

Early in the first day of the program, we were asked to write a personal story of how gun violence had touched our lives. I had become involved in gun violence work because of the Newtown shootings, but the question invited me to try to remember other attacks that had touched me deeply.

I thought of the attack on the North Valley Jewish Community Center in Los Angeles in 1999, with its riveting photographic image of a long line of small children being led across the street to safety, tiny hands clasped in terror. I thought of the spate of suicides among students at the high school my daughter attended, and of the recent murder of Reuven Rahamim at his workplace in Minneapolis. Not coincidentally, in these incidents, the victims were Jews, or schoolmates of my daughter's.

But in the silence, as people in the room put their thoughts on paper, I knew that the African-American clergy at my table had a radically different experience of the exercise than I did. The pastor to my right shrugged his shoulders in frustration, muttering, "One story? How could I possibly choose one story?"

As the days of the meeting unfolded, this place became my own story of gun violence. Sharing meals and conversation, tears, laughter and prayer with my African-American colleagues, I glimpsed their everyday experience of gun violence. I heard again and again that these attacks were regular occurrences in their ministry. Burying a young adult whose birth he had witnessed, over whose baptism she had officiated. Learning that a young man had been shot dead as he tried to reach the church for safety. Grieving over families who had lost two, three, even four children to gun violence. Resolving to risk their own lives, walking gang-dominated streets late at night to communicate their concern and solidarity with the families of their community.

I thought we had come to talk about Newtown, and the tragic opportunity it presented to promote sensible gun violence prevention measures in our country. My colleagues grieved the horror of Newtown as I did. But for them and their communities, Newtown happens every week, if not every day.

My head ached and I felt physically ill as we learned more about the problem of urban gun violence. 30,000 Americans killed in domestic violence each year, half of them young people. For perspective, 12,000-13,000 people die in terrorist activists all over the world each year. Approximately 60,000 people have died since the violence began in Syria, and most of the world considers that a massacre. My mind struggled to absorb the basic facts: more than 80 people (half of them young people) die every day of gun violence in the United States.

Horror and pain turned to confusion and shame. How could I not have known or understood the breadth and depth of the problem of urban violence, an epidemic by any standard? Surely, I had been dimly aware of the problem, but for a combination of reasons -- distance (not in my part of town), overwhelm, and denial, among them -- I had not attended to this problem. Not my issue.

Newtown woke me up. As a parent, the death of 20 small children broke open my heart and mind, so that I had no choice but to become engaged with the issue. But like the other horrific mass shootings in recent memory (Columbine, Tucson, Aurora, Oak Creek), the setting was not the inner city, and the victims were white. Coincidence? Or have I, like so much of white America, conveniently placed my attention elsewhere while blood ran in the streets of our cities?

In the weeks since the conference, my thoughts have returned again and again to the Jewish teaching on *piku'ach nefesh*—the imperative to save life, even when this necessitates violating Jewish law (with only three exceptions). One of the classical texts on *piku'ach nefesh* specifically and urgently teaches that if a child's life can be saved, one must violate Shabbat, as soon as possible, without tarrying to ask a rabbinic court's opinion.[79] No less than four times during this brief text, we read "the sooner the better." We are forbidden to tarry when children's lives are at stake, even if the life-saving activity has other consequences.

The message of this text could not be more clear. It is time to act to save the lives of the children endangered every day by gun violence. The sooner the better. May it be so.

---

[79] Babylonian Talmud, Yoma 84b

WHEN GOD CRIES[80]

Rabbi Jesse Olitzky

The Sabbath is meant to be a day of rest, a day of peace. That is why in Hebrew we say Shabbat Shalom. Yet, following the terrible mass shooting tragedy at Sandy Hook Elementary School in Newtown, Connecticut on Friday that left twenty young children murdered in cold blood, this past Shabbat was emotionally draining for so many of us. Many asked, "Where is God?" This is a question that we often ask at times of tragedy, inexplicable moments of darkness.

The answer: God is here, with us. As we watch the news and wail, as our tears drip into puddles on the front page, God is also crying. God is right by our side, in horror, in shock, in disbelief, crying. Through the Prophet Isaiah God cries out:

> Turn away from me and let me weep bitterly. Don't try to comfort me, for the destruction of my people.[81]

God cries. The Omnipotent does not try and intervene. Rather, after giving us, God's children made in God's image, the blessing of responsibility, God cries. The mournful book of Lamentations tells of the tragedy of the destruction of the Temple in Jerusalem. In the

---

[80] This sermon was first delivered by Rabbi Olitzky on December 17, 2012 in at the Jacksonville Jewish Center in Jacksonville, Florida.

[81] Isaiah 22:4

midrash, God cries out. Trying to comprehend the violence and hate that destroyed a symbol of peace and unity, God bemoans:

> Woe is Me for My house, My children – where are you? My priests, where are you? Those who love Me, where are you?[82]

God cries with us. God feels helpless, just as we do.

As parents, some of us just wanted to curl up in a ball, hide the news from our children, and protect them from the darkness of this world. Our hearts broke upon hearing the name of each child, so young, so innocent, like our matriarch Sarah, who, according to tradition, died of a broken heart, after she thought that her one and only child was no longer living. Others among us refuse to accept this as reality, waiting to wake up from this nightmare.

In the immediate aftermath of this tragedy, many parents suggested that we should simply go home, pray, and hug our children. This is what I did. This is what I always do at the end of the day. I squeeze my daughter tight and beg God to protect her. Then I ask, "what can I do to protect her?" That is when I remember that I cannot hug her all the time. I cannot permanently shield her from harm's way. I must take responsibility to make this world a better place, a safer place, for her.

On Sunday evening at the Newtown Interfaith Memorial Service, President Barack Obama shared these words:

> We are all parents. They are all our children. This is our first task, caring for our children. If we don't get that right, we don't get anything right. That is how as a society we will be judged. Are we prepared to say that we are powerless in the face of such carnage?

Are we prepared to take responsibility? Are we prepared to take action and to prevent such acts from happening ever again? We must not sit idly by and watch God's children destroy each other. The late Rabbi Abraham Joshua Heschel, a leader in social justice, taught

> Above all, the prophets remind us of the moral state of a people: Few are guilty, but all are responsible.

---

[82] Lamentations Rabbah

There have been calls for increased awareness and assistance for those suffering from mental illness. This is necessary.

However, so is stricter gun control. I am responsible. You are responsible. We are responsible. Some focus on the second amendment, the right to bear arms. This right is supposed to ensure our safety. Such a right has only caused more danger in our society. There have been fourteen mass shootings in this past year alone. Stricter laws as well as an increase in mental healthcare will help prevent lethal weapons from legally ending up in the hands of those who should not be carrying them. Our children's right to a future full of opportunity takes precedent over our right to bear arms. We are responsible. We must wipe away our tears and make a change so that God too can stop crying.

Rabbi Heschel also noted, reflecting on his march for civil rights from Selma to Montgomery, that:

> ...legs are not lips and walking is not kneeling. And yet our legs uttered songs. Even without words, our march was worship. I felt my legs were praying.

Let us take action. Let us pray with our feet.

Until this moment of change takes place, I continue to pray to the Holy One, asking God to protect all of our children. Quoting the words of the Priestly Benediction, traditionally said by parents to their children on Sabbath eve:

> May God bless you and protect you. May God's Face radiate upon you and be gracious unto you. May God lift up God's Face unto you and grant you peace.[83]

May we, made in the Divine image, help ensure such blessing, such protection, such grace, and such peace through our actions. We are God's messengers. When we act, God acts. When we sit around in disbelief and refuse to do nothing, God cries.

---

83 Numbers 6:26

May we mourn all those lives lost in Newtown and may their memories be for a blessing.

GOD FULL OF MERCY

Rabbi Ben Goldstein

Today I find myself thinking of the words of the great Israeli poet Yehuda Amichai z"l:

> God-Full-of-Mercy, the prayer for the dead. If God was not full of mercy, Mercy would have been in the world, not just in Him.

Too often we are awakened to news of violence and death. Too often we are left with bloodshed and murder. We wonder when it will end. We wonder what a man could be thinking to intentionally inflict so much hurt on people he doesn't even know. We wonder how a God who created the beauty of nature could allow evil and destruction to mar his beautiful canvas. The red streams created by nonsensical acts leave us wondering about God's benevolence or lack thereof.

What is there left for us to do when the news makes us want to cry and cover our ears to pain and suffering? What recourse do we have to battle the pessimism and bleakness that we feel when we see these stories? How do we keep the darkness at bay?

Some people give in to anger. They divide humanity into categories that seem to make it easier to navigate their lives. There are those that are good and those that are bad. There is the "us" and those who want to hurt "us." They turn to their leaders and blame this policy or that policy, "why didn't you keep us safer" they beg.

We cannot judge those who respond with anger, those who cry for vengeance. We cannot judge them any more than we can judge those who give into the sadness and devastation that they feel. When we hear their words, let us listen to their anguish and fear. Let us overcome the hatred and the rage and begin to heal the terror and devastation.

We all cope differently.

We all find ways of reaching out to catch that light that will shine through the darkness that surrounds us. I don't know what helps other people face the depravity of life and Man. For me, all I can do is pray. I pray to a God whose attributes I do not know. I pray to a universe whose meaning is beyond me. I pray that all life has meaning. I pray that my life can serve a purpose. I pray that the lives of those who have been taken from us will live on. I pray that God exists and can hear my prayers.

> God Full of Mercy:
>
> Have mercy on those whose lives ended their before their times. Comfort those whose sobs ring in our ears. Let them know that they are not alone.
>
> God, guide us through this difficult time as we fumble our way through the darkness.
>
> Help your children whose hope has been diminished. Show us that goodness and beauty can triumph. Bless us to bring light into this world. Bless us to do the work that needs to be done.
>
> May we be blessed to do God's work and may God be blessed through the work of our hands.

Gun Violence in Our Country: A Crisis for Every Single American[84]

Rabbi Aaron Alexander

I'm astonished that powerful public voices are still chastising gun-violence prevention advocates in this country by claiming that they are using the Sandy Hook shooting as a manipulative tool to backhandedly rid our country of guns. It's not helpful. It is also unclear how reacting to trauma by working to subvert further trauma is anything but just. One may not like their proposed answers, but let's not attack the integrity of the response. There is simply no (credible or supported) movement to "grab all the guns," but rather, an essential debate on how to best uplift public safety for everybody while still taking Second Amendment rights seriously.

I'd like to offer at least one reason why I won't stop talking about gun violence, specifically Newtown and its watershed implications.

I recently attended a multi-faith clergy gathering in Washington, D.C., on the topic of gun violence in our society. I expected we would focus our collective energy in bringing a religious voice to the sorts of common-sense gun control measures being hotly debated across America. To a certain extent, we did, and I am overflowing with statistics and facts about modern weaponry, beyond what I ever imagined I would know.

[84] This essay first appeared on Rabbi Alexander's HuffPost blog on Feb. 14, 2013

But I quickly realized this unique gathering offered something different. When asked to share just one personal story of gun violence, I looked across the table from me toward two pastors, who looked somewhat confused. "*One story?*" "*Really?*" "*ONLY one story?!*"

When asked to share one personal story of gun violence, I looked across th table from me toward two pastors, who looked somewhat confused. "One story?" "Really?" "*ONLY one story?!*"

Reality began to set in. It occurred to me that most of the clergy in this particular room would officiate at more funerals of gun-violence victims under the age of 25 in a month, than I would even attend in my lifetime. My blinders began to lift. Was this my "Moses comes down from the mountain" moment?

In perhaps the most suspenseful story in the Torah, Moses, after pleading successfully with God to spare the Israelite's lives after the Golden Calf debacle[85], sees for himself the raucous actions of his clan and cannot contain his anger and outrage. He crashes to the ground the sacred and precious gift he had just received from God, the Ten Commandments.

But is this public display of frustration an acceptable leadership paradigm to celebrate? Isn't this kind of emotional response exactly what we strive to keep out of the public sphere?

In a boundary-pushing rabbinic response, the Talmud radically reconfigures God's reaction to Moses' shattering of the tablets as a sign of respect, and admiration. When God directs Moses to construct the second set of tablets, two "seemingly" superfluous words appear at the end of the verse:

> The Lord said to Moses: "Carve two tablets of stone like the first, and I will inscribe upon the tablets the words that were on the first tablets, *which you shattered*."[86]

---

[85] Exodus 32:11-14
[86] Exodus 34:1

Why did God feel the need to remind Moses that he broke the first set of tablets? You'd think that memory would still be quite fresh. The rabbinic response:

> Resh Lakish says: There are times when the shattering of Torah is actually its foundation, as it is written: "which you shattered (*asher shibarta*)." God said to Moses, "Way to go, you broke them! (*Yasher Koach She-shibarta!*)"[87]

Resh Lakish imagined that God recognized some events so jarring and disruptive that the only authentic response is outrage, astonishment and direct action -- even if something important is lost along the way. Yes, even the Ten Commandments, wholly Divine, became secondary to human behavior in this moment.

In fact, this raw response is the essential stuff of transformation. It is only when we tangibly experience the pain, denigration and even failure of others -- to the realistic extent possible -- that we can become catalysts for real change. This powerful sense of empathy links us to their stories and begs us to responsible participation in the unfolding narrative that surrounds us.

This remarkable passage and its message speak truth for so many of us right now. It directly addresses why so many voices are loudly gathering to challenge the unnecessary legislative and financial gridlock that threatens our communities as thousands of lives are continually being lost. It is why the NRA's out-of-touch leadership is rightly demonized throughout vast sectors of society.

The Newtown tragedy -- and its "*that could have been in my neighborhood*" sensation -- is waking us up to the fact that Sandy Hook happens each day in this country. It has cracked open a nation's heart such that our eyes may finally witness that which is directly in front of us: in our towns, throughout all neighborhoods in our cities, across our nation. It is Aurora and Sandy Hook, but so much more. It is about angry men and vulnerable women, adults and children, suburban schools and inner-city playgrounds, gangs and suicides. It is in Newtown and New Orleans, Chicago and Columbine, and Oak Creek and Oakland. And it occurs several times a day.

---

[87] Babylonian Talmud, Menachot 99a-b

As an entire nation we are now sufficiently unsettled and broken, and we ourselves must continue the process of tablet shattering.

Of saying, "*Enough*!"

Of saying, "My entire country is my community and all in its borders deserve the opportunity to live in peace and safety."

As Dr. Martin Luther King Jr.'s eternal message teaches:

> "We are caught in an inescapable network of mutuality, tied in a single garment of destiny. Whatever affects one directly, affects all indirectly."[88]

If you, like me, are just waking up, now is the time to make your voice heard. If you advocate for stronger and common sense gun-control measures, call your elected officials or sign a petition.

If you are a member of a faith community, invite your congregation to join communities across the country in a "Gun Violence Prevention Sabbath."

If you think stronger gun control is the wrong direction, you still have a voice and moral imperative in the gun violence conversation that goes beyond the Second Amendment. Please assert it. Support proven life-saving programs all across our country with donations, like the Boston Ten Point Coalition or the Institute For the Study and Practice of Non-Violence or the nation-wide Ceasefire programs.

And finally, average members of the NRA, please notify your leadership that they likely no longer speak on your behalf, but only obscure our national dilemma with duplicitous smokescreen tactics.

Now is the time.

---

88 Letter From a Birmingham Jail

To Stay Awake

Rabbi Noah Z. Farkas

There are times when life chooses our topics. There are times when news of the day keeps us up at night with worry for the families and empathy for the victims. It is at these times that we are provoked to ask deep and irrepressible questions about the foundations of our society. It has been said that insomnia is a Jewish trait. The philosopher Emmanuel Levinas wrote of the phenomenon of being jolted awake into the unsettling present as a "gathering into being or presence where at a certain depth of vigilance, vigilance has to clothe itself in justice." When we see the horrors of violence, of children murdered in school, of husbands and wives murdered at home, of friends shot while enjoying a summer's day - we must surrender the possibility of humanity. Rather, we must wake up to our human potential. As someone once noted, "The Jews can't sleep and they won't let the world sleep."

When the news of Sandy Hook began to spread over the internet, I got the same feeling I felt fourteen years earlier when the news of Columbine spread and the same feeling I had when, in my community, Buford O. Furrow, Jr. walked into the Jewish Community Center and shot five people with a semi-automatic weapon. I called my wife and all I could say was, "the kinder, the kinder." I experienced on that day, not for the first time, the feeling of Levinas' prophetic insomnia. An incision was made into the fabric of my reality that cried out to me like's God's scream that awakened the first human heart to justice in the Book of Genesis. "What have you done? Lo, your brother's blood cries out to Me from the ground!"[89]

The next morning we held several meetings with parents in our schools to give them room to process the experience. Of the varied responses, many included questions about our own children's safety. Do we have enough armed guards on campus? Are the fences high enough? Are the gates tough enough to keep the bad guys out? I understood their concerns. As a parent of three young children I share their fear for my little ones. Yet when our tradition sees the insanity that seems to teem just under the crust of the world it demands that we must make order out of chaos and bring light to the darkness.

After the destruction of the Second Temple, Rabbi Shimon bar Yochai saw the trappings of the Roman world with its streets and aqueducts, its politicians and its spies. The rabbi with his son Elazar fled to seclusion of the cave where they buried their bodies in sand up to their heads and did nothing but study the inner dimensions of the Torah. They stayed in that cave for twelve years praying, fasting, and studying. Once they heard that the Roman emperor had died, the pair descended from the cave and found Jews sowing seeds and plowing rows for the harvest. The two scholars became enraged and shouted:

> "You are giving up eternal life for the sake of the mundane!" At that moment, wherever they cast their eyes became engulfed with the flame of their fury. Out of heaven came God's voice who said, "Did you come to destroy my world*? Get back into the cave!*"[90]

When tragedy strikes, there is a deep temptation to retreat into the cave of our own family, of our own friends, of our own clan. For a short time we displace the feelings of confusion and grief that fester in our hearts by seeking refuge in the comfortable. We see our sacred spaces as sanctuaries - a place away from the world where the exhaustion from the chaos can be slept off. Such is the temptation to go back to sleep after a hard night.

Judaism pushes against this idea with all its heart, with all its might, and with all its soul. Ours is, as Rabbi Harold Schulweis teaches, a

---

[89] Gen.4:8

[90] Babylonian Talmud, Shabbat 33b

global faith. The first eleven chapters of the Torah knows nothing of Jews or Judaism. After the flood, still some ten generations before the birth of Abraham our father, God says to Noah, "For your own life-blood I require a reckoning; I will require it of every beast; of humanity too, will I require a reckoning, of every person and his fellow...for in God's image did God make humanity."[91]

God's initial covenant is with all that live. Life itself is Godly. All that is from the ant to the Tree of Life itself comes from the same earth and share the same covenant to be fertile and flourish. Murder then, is the highest sin, for it defaces the imprint of the Creator.

Mt. Sinai is the dawning of the Israelite nation as a free people. Taken from captivity and brought through the sea, the tribes of Israel stand as witnesses for themselves and their children and their children's children - for an everlasting covenant between God and the Jewish people. Jews must see themselves at this moment, always with their friends and family. So much does the moment of revelation play on the Jewish heart that when a newly converted Jew-By-Choice comes into the community it is not unusual for someone to say, "I saw you at Sinai." Yet Sinai is not only a particularistic revelation. God did not speak to our nation alone. The Heavenly Voice stretches beyond the boundaries of the mountain. The rabbis teach that at the moment when God gave the sacred tablets to Moses the entire earth shuddered and all of creation stood still to listen to God's disclosure to the whole of earth.

The Midrash teaches that the Divine Writ was carved through the stone on "both sides of the tablet." Thus, from any angle, the Ten Commandments speak to the universal heart. These laws are the bridge between the particular and the universal, between individual and community, between the Jew and Gentile. God's covenant with Noah, symbolized through the rainbow, refracts again through the dual prism of the tablets. Each side of the carved stone shines forth with this deepest of injunctions. Moses could see it, the Israelites could see it, and all of creation could see it. Thus, "Do not murder" is both a particular rule of our nation and a universal commandment to all. To vitiate another life through an act of violence, then, is not only to break our own laws, but rips open the very foundation of life

---

[91] Gen.9:5-7

itself.

Our greatness as a religion is in our gifts of compassion and responsibility and not in our building the so the wonders of the world. Mt. Sinai teaches to be a Jew is to resist either/or categories of thinking. The rabbis teach that we support the poor of the Gentile. We visit their sick. We mourn their dead *"mipnei darkei shalom,"* for the ways of peace.[92]

Every Jews has universal responsibilities, because one cannot be a Jew until one affirms being human first. The pathways of peace can only be trodden through the gates that our open to all of humanity.

"Few are guilty" Rabbi Abraham Joshua Heschel wrote, "but all are responsible." We are responsible to protect one another, to heal one another, and to respond to the tragedies of the world with a sense of wakefulness; with a vigilance clothed in justice as God's allies to make the world whole and living.

---

[92] Mishna Gittin 5:8

The Ten Commandments and Gun Violence

Rabbi David Kaiman

In my part of the country it is not uncommon to read a letter-to-the-editor or local news article defending the display of The Ten Commandments on some public square or courthouse. Usually it is under the guise of demanding to practice faith openly or asserting an opinion that this country was founded on biblical principles. When we read those famous words in Exodus in the synagogue I wonder about the overall direction and theme of these Ten Commandments. What is special about these ten statements? What lesson are we to learn from this collection of laws that seems so central for so many?

The definitive voice in the beginning of these ten statements is clearly a voice of faith and loyalty. It is the voice of established authority that strikes us, as it did the ancient Israelites, with the sense that there is a cosmic seriousness to THESE commands as opposed to the rulings of some mortal king. The voice of The Ten Commandments turns quickly to the practicalities of life as we learn about organizing holy time. That is meant to be a reminder that we live in a world that we did not create and we live in imitation of the celestial creator.

But then these commandments take a radical turn for with the rest of the commands we hear clear statements of moral direction. We are to honor parents and refrain from theft , murder, adultery, false witness and jealousy.

It seems to me that in this one unit that we call The Ten Commandments we are given a dynamic message: We are to acknowledge that God has created a world for us that demands our appreciation and attention and as a result we are presented with legislation that is meant to create a world of morality and conscience. It is the voice of faith that compels us to find a way to create a system of justice and laws. And those laws are meant to guide us toward paths of civilized society.

Today we live in a world where violence threatens the innocent in every city of America. As a result of Sandy Hook we were shaken to discover that even middle class suburban children were not immune from a deranged man with an assault rifle. We have seen elected officials gunned down in public, theatre patrons subject to militia-style attacks and office personnel confronted by angry co-workers. Gun violence is rampant in inner city America and threatens every citizen. Additionally, the wide availability of weapons that have more power and deadly force has changed the landscape of consumer weaponry in a way that demands our attention like never before.

The religious response, as modeled in The Ten Commandments, is clear: If we are to have faith that there is a God of justice and lawfulness then we are obligated to extend the law to address the response of a society where gun violence is rampant. The foundation was set for us when The Ten Commandments used the religious context to establish lawful behavior between human beings. It is our faith that propels us to declare that murder, theft and adultery are crimes. It will be our faith that drives us to devise some system that addresses the kind of violence that results in the senseless murders that occur with assault-styled weapons.

But simply displaying a copy of The Ten Commandments seems to miss the point of a code of law. Guns, ammunition and cigarettes all come with adequate warnings of their lethality. In fact, I would argue that because The Ten Commandments are so specific to the Judeo-Christian traditions its display would only serve to alienate those who are already distant from their faith communities or who come from different traditions.

No, our most effective use of The Ten Commandments is not as a wall hanging or stone statue but rather as a model for writing clear legislation that unambiguously allows us to build a better, safer and more just world for our citizens.

Passover, Non-Violence and Gun Control[93]

Rabbi Aryeh Cohen

Google claims today that there are 1,790,000 websites that have the phrase "the meaning of the Exodus story." (By now probably more—including this one.) The Exodus, of course, has many meanings—and two major motion pictures. John Adams wanted the splitting of the Red Sea to be on the Great Seal of the newly minted United States of America. This plethora of interpretations should make one hesitate before offering new meanings to this ancient event which has inspired millions of people over millennia.

I want, instead, to resurrect an interpretation first offered 107 years ago in a small town in eastern Poland by a Rabbi whose name was Aharon Shmuel Tamares. Tamares pointed to an interesting detail in the Biblical story. After commanding the Israelites regarding the Passover sacrifice, and telling them that they need to put the blood of the sacrifice on their doorposts, and further telling them that He was going to kill all the Egyptian firstborns, God says: "None of you shall go outside the door of his house until morning."[94]

Tamares suggests that this detail is actually central to the story. In the retelling of the story at the annual seder, we read that God

[93] This piece originally appeared as part of *Open Zion* on the Daily Beast on Mar 25, 2013.
[94] Exodus 12:22

personally destroyed the Egyptians without outside aid—angel or human. Why didn't God empower the Israelites to wreak vengeance on their enemies who were evil people? This, then, is the meaning of the Exodus. God did not want Israel to witness the violence inflicted on the Egyptians so as to stop the cycle of violence. God knew, says Tamares, that all violence leads to more violence. The victim who takes up sword or fist will eventually become the predator—and the cycle will continue. In an attempt to stop the cycle, God did not allow the Israelites to be involved in this necessary violence, so as to stop the use of violence right then.

Well, this didn't work out as planned and violence continues (and victims daily become predators). However, every year when we celebrate the Exodus with the words "I, God wreaked vengeance on the Ancient Egyptians, I myself," we are challenged to renew our commitment to nonviolence—to recalling that violence is a tool that can only be used by God, if at all—because once used, it is always used again. A "good guy with a gun" does not stop "a bad guy with a gun," rather the "good guy" with the gun continues the cycle of violence and eventually becomes the bad guy. The only way to break the cycle is at the root. The only way to stop the bad guy is to make sure he does not have a gun.

In the current climate, where our Congress is debating whether or not to ban weapons of war from private ownership, we are far from this ideal situation. We cannot even agree that implements of violence whose only purpose is to kill many, many people do not have a place in our society. In this time when every week there are more victims of gun violence than there were in the Sandy Hook Elementary School on that tragic December day—we cannot even agree that violent intimate partners with restraining orders against them should surrender their weapons.

Passover is a time of transformation, hope, and redemption. To get from here to there—if there is a country, and ultimately perhaps a world without violence—we have to transform our culture. We have to pass laws that will ban the weapons of destruction, but we also must go after the gun industries whose sole product is death. There are some three hundred million guns in private hands. In order to deal with those guns we must change the gun cultures in this country. The urban gun culture and the rural gun culture. We must change our understanding of masculinity so that it doesn't necessitate violent resolutions to conflict. We must prize the first amendment and the speech it allows more than the second amendment and the speech it denies.

This is a tall order. It is a plan for years, not weeks or days. Yet in its time Biblical Egypt symbolized the regime that could not be changed. Passover reminds us that change is possible. The possibility to change an immovable culture is God working in the world. As a first step, perhaps we can agree that private citizens should not own weapons of war.

The Fifth Child[95]

Rabbi Joshua Hammerman

On Passover we read about the Four Children, each of whom approaches the seder experience from a different angle. We are called upon to explain the Exodus story in the manner most developmentally appropriate for each child.

The Fourth Child is arguably the most challenging one, since that child doesn't even know how to ask.

I propose that this year we add a Fifth Child, updating a custom used back in the heyday of the Soviet Jewry movement, and more recently as a stand-in for Gilad Shalit or those facing debilitating illness. But now we have a new Fifth Child. Alongside the one who does not know how to ask, we must now include the one who can't ask, not because she's stuck in a Gulag or Gazan prison, but because she's been killed, right here in America. This is the child whose inquisitive mind has been stilled forever by the magazines of a maniac's assault rifle, or by the single bullet of a parent's unlocked handgun, or at the hands of an abusive caregiver, or as the result of incessant bullying and unremitting cruelty.

Deeply embedded in the Exodus narrative is a subtext, the idea that Egypt is not merely a place but also a metaphor. Rabbinic wisdom relates the Hebrew word for Egypt, *Mitzrayim*, to the term for "tight place," in the sense of one's being constricted. In this literary

[95] A version of this introduction appeared in the New York Jewish Week on march 19, 2013 and appears here with the author's permission.

interpretation, the shackles of slavery are a reflection of our own narrow-mindedness. If Egypt is a metaphor, then we are enslaved not to Pharaoh, but to our own prejudice and anger — and to our pervasive culture of violence.

There are far too many Fifth Children out there, and we've allowed that to happen. We have produced a society where child sacrifice is once again in vogue. That child, though now residing in our cemeteries, deserves a place at this year's table.

In this way, Passover is exceptionally relevant in the wake of Newtown. It points to the anger and violence that we are combating (I wish we could get beyond military terms.) in our society and within our hearts as well. The current struggle is about firearms for sure, but it's also about our combustible souls.

According to Slate, in the nearly three months from Newtown to March 7, guns killed 2,659 Americans. That running tally is incomplete, but it is illustrative, and that tally includes nearly 200 teens and children. So in the three months since the children died at Newtown, there have been effectively ten more Sandy Hooks in this country.

And still, Congress hems and haws.

Military assault weapons and high capacity magazines continue to be freely available in a civilian society where they serve absolutely no good purpose. Even after Newtown, the best Washington appears able to do is come up with a plan to enhance the system of background checks. Our reps appear stuck in these narrow straits of Egypt, addicted to our culture of violence, bound to these narrow straits by political arm twisting and pressure lobbying. It seems as if our representatives are voting, metaphorically, with a gun to their heads. There is no other way to explain the lack of outrage and moral resolve in preventing future Newtowns and eliminating the 10th plague of gun violence from our society.

The sage Hillel famously said, "If not now, when?" In Congress, prodded by the NRA, that rabbinic call to arms (oops) has been transformed into a sullen teenager's "If not now, whenever!" I have news for everyone: this is the "now" that Hillel was talking about. If large magazines and assault weapons aren't curtailed now, they never will be. And if they aren't, more children will die — and their blood will be on our hands.

I was one of 4,000 clergy to sign a letter written by Newtown clergy imploring senators to vote for strong legislation to prevent gun violence. Four thousand! In this country it's hard to get 4,000 clergy to agree that the sky is blue, but the cause of ending gun violence mends denominational differences even as it rends families and communities apart.

Ending this plague is the cry of our generation, a moral imperative and ITAL a Jewish imperative. It is universal and particularistic. Before Newtown there was Northridge — the JCC shooting in 1999. As a Jew, I care about all innocent human beings, but I also know that my own people are especially threatened by a gun-running culture that allows, through gun show loopholes, for white supremacists like Buford Furrow Jr. to procure unconscionably lethal weapons without a problem and blast 70 gunshots into a JCC complex with the intent of killing lots of Jewish kids.

So this Passover, we need to wonder about who is not at the table. The children of Newtown need a voice. So do the four children of Shirley Chambers, the Chicago mother who lost all four of her children to gun violence. All human life is of equal value. Let all those children now become the Fifth Child at our seders, all children, everywhere, who have fallen victim to our society's gun-sanity. They are the child who cannot ask because we have allowed them to be killed on our watch.
We are killing our own children because we are letting them be killed.

This crucial issue is the real "right to life" movement, for no matter what our beliefs regarding the origin or end of life, everyone agrees that first graders have a right to live.

Together, let us search for a common path that will lead us from Egypt, from the scourge of violence that has plagued us for far too long.

Karpas -Drenched in Tears: A reflection on Gun Violence in our Society for the Passover Seder

Rabbi Ron Fish

One of the ways in which we tell the story of the Exodus at our Seders is through silence. In addition to all the singing and talking, the studying and debating, we also use simple acts of solidarity with those who suffer to speak for us. We don't just eat Matzah because we left Egypt in haste. We open the Seder story by looking at the unleavened bread and we quietly remember this as the bread of affliction. We don't just think of the bitterness of those whose lives were stripped of their humanity. We are asked to try to literally taste the bitterness of our ancestors' pain.

And we also taste their tears.

The salty water into which we dip our green vegetables is a reminder of the anguish of slavery as it stole from generations their youth, their hopefulness, their fresh beginnings. In this moment, eating the first food of our Seder meal, we identify with the senseless tragedy of babies and lives lost, drown in hate. You can almost hear the muffled cries of mothers and survivors, themselves soaked in the salty pain of those left behind.

This year at my Seder I will join in the pain, the anguish, the tears of those who have buried loved ones due to gun violence.

This year at my Seder, as I dip my parsley into salt water, I will reflect on the immeasurable waste of so many lives all around us.

This year, at my Seder, about 20 miles away from Newtown, CT- I will shudder. Thinking of the insanity of our nation's culture of violence, I will be left speechless. For all the pious talk of the sanctity of life, my silence at the Seder will reflect the silence of our society- even now. We remain reluctant to speak the obvious truth- 30,000 lives lost annually to gun violence is an abomination.
At my Seder I will taste the tears yet to be shed by those who will next be bereaved. Who will it be? You? Me?

At my Seder I will recall that hope can be drown in pain and anguish and loss.

And at my Seder I will remember that we can pass through these waters, as we have in times past, and make our world better.

But first... we must make their tears our own.

AFTERWORD to the First Edition

A JUST DAY

Teny Oded Gross

Being a former Israeli Army sergeant has helped me understand and respond to violence. I've been both a victim of violence through the legacy of the Holocaust and then was top dog when it came to the Palestinians. I'm part of the weak and part of the strong; that's a very humbling experience.

I try to see things through the eyes of the kids and through the eyes of the police. Keeping those tensions in my head reminds me that while we're really good at going in and intervening, the work of really transforming someone takes a longer time. This work will focus on youth development. It will take thousands of interactions. It's all about exposure.

What would many of those caught up in the epidemic of Gun Violence be they'd grown up in an affluent suburb? A jock, a star athlete, captain of the team. Kids who go to Harvard are not passive wimps—they're very aggressive, very driven. But for street kids, that sense of power too often comes through mowing people down. I think what we're pushing for is a more evolved form of aggression.

We need more civilized behavior. Many sectors fail to provide a civilized example. The way some athletes, politicians, business leaders, cops and teachers talk today is amazing. Whether in public service or private business, many of us have a sense of entitlement. How then can we expect our kids to be polite, have a sense of direction? We have to make it cool to be civilized.

And whether you believe in God or not is not critical. I believe that people are capable of living up to their potential if given love and attention and opportunities. I connect with communities of faith because they are dedicated around principles that I agree with—that every human life is worth something and worth doing something about.

The easy response to crime is to lock up the troublemakers, but preventing crimes and rehabilitating offenders—"recycling human capital"—saves millions of dollars. We won't get what you want by forcing our will. We cannot talk about kindness. It's got to be demonstrated every day, all the time.

This is a struggle that is critical for us as a society. If the Jewish Community gets more involved we will have a new, just day in America.

AFTERWORD TO THE SECOND EDITION

Blood Upon Our House[96]

Dr. Erica Brown

"You shall not bring blood upon your house." (Deuteronomy 24:8)

One morning a few weeks ago, my husband walked into our bedroom and said, "There's been a shooting at University of Maryland." Not yet knowing the details but knowing one fact — our daughter is a student there — I did what every parent would do. I closed my eyes, held my breath and called her cellphone. She answered. I breathed. She had just heard the news and was about to call to let us know she was OK.

But all is not OK — not OK on the UMD campus, where there have been five gun-related incidents around campus in the past three weeks - and not OK in this country where the gun control issue has been reduced to a matter of partisan politics and incivility. We can't even talk about it. The "loaded" debates are blinding us to the stark reality: too many people with mental illness and criminal records have access to guns. The UMD graduate student shot and killed one student, wounded another and killed himself. Next to his body police found a bag containing a fully-loaded, semi-automatic Uzi, several rounds of ammunition, a machete and a baseball bat.

---

[96] A version of this introduction appeared in the New York Jewish Week on February 26, 2013 and appears here with the author's permission.

Jewish law forbids the selling of weapons to those suspected of using them for criminal ends:

> One should not sell them either weapons or accessories of weapons, nor should one grind any weapon for them, nor may one sell them stocks, chains or ropes.[97]

But we don't have to go that far. The Talmud admonishes us not to keep a bad dog or a broken ladder at home because these can accidentally endanger family or visitors. In the Talmud, a hole in a public space must be covered lest anyone come close and trip into it as a result. We must put a parapet around a flat roof in case someone comes too near the edge and falls off. Precautions focus our attention on the issue of safety in the home. A gun is an object that kills. It does not belong in a house.

In this new universe of added security with a gun in every hand becoming a new American mantra like Hoover's "chicken in every pot," everyone is a potential suspect. *Is this the world we want?*

You can counter this by marshaling the Talmudic permission to kill someone who is pursuing you in murder. In Exodus 22:1, we even grant permission to strike a thief dead who is discovered breaking into one's home; the murderer is blameless. Since the thief would likely kill the homeowner to escape being found, the homeowner acted in self-defense. This is true for American law as well.

But if we go down this road, we have to imagine a world where everyone — even children — have to be armed to stop someone else who is armed. It's not only about owning a gun. It's about knowing how to use it expertly and having it at precisely the moment when bedlam strikes. "*Ain l'davar sof*," we say in Hebrew, "To this, there is no end."

---

[97] Babylonian Talmud, Avodah Zarah 15b

And in this new universe of added security with a gun in every hand becoming a new American mantra like Hoover's "chicken in every pot," everyone is a potential suspect. Is this the world we want?

Contrast this to a Talmudic passage about Shabbat. One "must not go out with a sword, bow, shield, or spear."[98] The sacredness of Shabbat cannot be marred by any instrument of violence. One sage counters that these implements are merely decorative. But others disagree citing the famous verse from Isaiah: "They will beat their swords into ploughshares and their spears into pruning-knives..."[99]

Gun control should be the Jewish cause of our time.

If Shabbat is truly holy to us then aspire to the vision of Isaiah. Put the weapons away. Many have the custom — as our family does — not to make a blessing on challah in the presence of the knife blade. Blessings and knives just don't go together.

Gun control should be the Jewish cause of our time. Our children should inherit a world where they feel safe enough to walk on a college quad without fear. They should feel safe enough to go to elementary school. But we are simply not outraged. We have come to accept murder rampages as a reality of everyday American life. If we believe that every legal mandate and mitzvah must be put aside to preserve life, then we are not fighting hard enough. We have not internalized the most basic Jewish impulse — that we are created in God's image and must preserve and sustain the godliness in all of humanity. We cannot stand by the blood of our brothers and sisters. Check Leviticus 19:16.

I write this not because I am a Democrat or a Republican, an NRA member or a pacifist. I write this because I am a mother, and I am a proud American, and I am a committed Jew. *And I cannot bear to see any more blood upon our house.*

---

98 Babylonian Talmud, Shabbat 63a

99 Isaiah 2:3-4

CONTRIBUTORS

Rabbi Aaron Alexander is Associate Dean of the Ziegler School of Rabbinic Studies at American Jewish University in Los Angeles where he teaches rabbinic literature and Jewish law. He currently serves on the Committee for Jewish and Standards of the Conservative Movement.

Rabbi David Baum received his rabbinic ordination and master's degree in Jewish education from the Jewish Theological Seminary in 2009. He serves as rabbi of Congregation Shaarei Kodesh in Boca Raton, Florida, sits on the Rabbinical Assembly's Social Justice Commission and serves as president of the Southeast Region of the Rabbinical Assembly.

Rabbi Shalom Bochner is the Director of Alma Retreats based in Berkeley, CA. He has 24 years' experience providing meaningful Jewish education and ritual leadership in a wide variety of settings including synagogues, Hillel, summer camps, youth groups, and day schools. He enjoys working with the full range of Jewish movements and expressions.

Rabbi Robyn Fryer Bodzin is spiritual leader of Israel Center of Conservative Judaism in New York City. She is active in her local PICO affiliate, Queens Congregations United for Action.

Rabbi Sharon Brous was recognized as the most influential Rabbi in the United States in 2013 by Newsweek and the Daily Beast, and as one of the Forward's 50 most influential American Jews. In 2013 Brous blessed the President and Vice President at the Inaugural National Prayer Service. She sits on the faculty of the Hartman Institute-North America, Wexner Heritage and REBOOT. She serves on the board of Teruah-The Rabbinic Call to Human Rights, is a rabbinic advisor to American Jewish World Service and Bend the Arc. She received the Lives of Commitment Award from Auburn Theological Seminary, was a JWI Woman to Watch and was the inaugural recipient of the Inspired Leadership Award from the Jewish Community Foundation of Los Angeles.

Dr. Erica Brown is a writer and educator who works as the scholar-in-residence for The Jewish Federation of Greater Washington and consults with for the Jewish Agency and other Jewish non-profits. Her most recent books are *Happier Endings: A Meditation on Life and Death* and *Leadership in the Wilderness: Authority and Anxiety in the Book of Numbers.* Erica writes a monthly column for The New York Jewish Week and the website Psychology Today and writes a weekly column for JTA on Jewish leadership. A faculty member of the Wexner Foundation, an Avi Chai Fellow, winner of the Ted Farber Professional Excellence Award, recipient of the 2009 Covenant Award for her work in education, and winner of the 2011 Bernie Reisman Award for Jewish Communal Service (Hornstein Jewish Professional Leadership Program, Brandeis University), Erica has degrees from Yeshiva University, University of London, Harvard University and Baltimore Hebrew University. She lectures widely on subjects of Jewish interest and leadership and writes a weekly internet essay called "Weekly Jewish Wisdom." She tweets daily on one page of the Talmud at @DrEricaBrown and tweets an inspirational quote or question called Happier Days.

Rabbi Dr. Aryeh Cohen is the Professor of Rabbinic Literature at the Ziegler School of Rabbinic Studies of the American Jewish University. He is the author, most recently, of Justice in the City: An Argument from the Sources of Rabbinic Judaism (Academic Studies Press, 2011). A past president of the Progressive Jewish Alliance, Rabbi Cohen is currently a board member of Bend the Arc: A Jewish Partnership for Justice, T'ruah: The Rabbinic Call for Human Rights, and Clergy and Laity United for Economic Justice-Los Angeles. Dr. Cohen was ordained as a Rabbi by the Ziegler School in 2010, and immediately following his ordination, he officiated at a bris, performed a wedding, and was arrested in a civil disobedience action in solidarity with the Los Angeles Hyatt Hotel workers.

Rabbi Gary S. Creditor has been an American Jewish leader for over 35 years, participating on countless boards and communal agencies, Jewish, interfaith, and civic. Rabbi Creditor was tapped by Governor Kaine to participate in the memorial program for the students and faculty who died as victims of Gun Violence at Virginia Tech. A member of the international Rabbinical Assembly of America, the Washington Board of Rabbis, and New York Board of Rabbis, Rabbi Creditor was ordained by the Jewish Theological Seminary of America, the world-wide center for Conservative Judaism. In 2003 he received his Doctorate from J.T.S. recognizing more than 25 years of Rabbinic service.

Rabbi Menachem Creditor serves as the spiritual leader of Congregation Netivot Shalom in Berkeley, CA. Named by *Newsweek* as one of the top Rabbis in America (2013), he is a published author, recording artist, teacher and activist who has spent time working in Ghana with American Jewish World Service and in the White House with the PICO Network to amplify the prophetic Jewish voice in the world. A frequent speaker on Jewish Leadership and Literacy in communities around the United States and Israel, he serves on many boards, including serving as chair of Bay Area Masorti, on the Executive Council of the Rabbinical Assembly, and on the Chancellor's Rabbinic Cabinet for the Jewish Theological Seminary of America. He blogs at menachemcreditor.org and is a regular contributor to the Huffington Post.

Rabbi Amy Eilberg is the first woman ordained as a Conservative rabbi by the Jewish Theological Seminary of America. After many years of working in pastoral care, hospice and spiritual direction, she has turned her attention to interfaith dialogue, communal conflict within the Jewish community, and Israeli-Palestinian grassroots reconciliation efforts. She is at work on a book on Judaism and peacemaking, tentatively entitled, "From Enemy to Friend: The Jewish Practice of Sacred Peacebuilding."

Rabbi Noah Zvi Farkas is a rabbi at Valley Beth Shalom in Encino, CA, a faculty member of the Florence Melton Graduate Studies Program and a guest lecturer at the American Jewish University. Rabbi Farkas founded Netiya, a faith-based network that advances urban agriculture in synagogues, schools, and non-profit organizations in Los Angeles. Noah has appeared on NPR, and writes a monthly column, "Turning the Tables," for the Jewish Daily Forward. Rabbi Farkas' most recent book is "The Social Action Manual: Six Steps to Repairing the World." He can followed on Twitter at @RabbiNoah

Rabbi Ron Fish has served as rabbi of Congregation Beth El in Norwalk, CT since August 2001. Rabbi Fish was ordained in 1996 from the Jewish Theological Seminary of America. Rabbi Fish has served as the president of the Norwalk Clergy Association and was the first president of Rabbinic Council of Norwalk and Westport. He was the driving force behind a number of crucial communal projects such as Taste of Torah, an evening of learning involving the entire community. Rabbi Fish also headed the organization of a communal basic Judaism course involving rabbinic educators from the entire religious spectrum. In 2006 Rabbi Fish successfully organized a synagogue trip to Israel during the second Lebanon War. The trip was the subject of a documentary on American Jews' experiences in encountering Israel called Eyes Wide Open.

Rabbi Ben Goldstein is the spiritual leader of Temple Beth El Mekor Chayim in Cranford New Jersey. His passion for teaching Judaism led him to work internationally with American Jewish World Service and the Joint Distribution Center. Ben also spent three years as a spiritual counselor at Beit Teshuvah, a Los Angeles based residential treatment center for drug and alcohol addiction.

Teny Oded Gross is Executive Director of the Institute for the Study and Practice of Nonviolence, a pioneering organization that teaches the principles and practices of nonviolence locally, nationally and internationally. Its Nonviolence Streetworkers Program is widely recognized for stemming gang violence. The Institute employs approximately 45 staff, many of which are former gang members.

Rabbi Steven Greenberg Rabbi Steven Greenberg is a Senior Teaching Fellow at CLAL and Director of the CLAL Diversity Project. In 2001 he appeared in Trembling Before G-d, a documentary about gay and lesbian Orthodox Jews, and joined the film maker, Sandi DuBowski, carrying the film across the globe as a tool for dialogue. He is the author of the book, Wrestling with God and Men: Homosexuality in the Jewish Tradition, (University of Wisconsin Press) and currently a founder and co-director of Eshel, an Orthodox LGBT community support and education organization. He lives with his partner, Steven Goldstein and daughter, Amalia in Boston.

Rabbi Joshua Hammerman is the spiritual leader of Temple Beth El in Stamford, CT. He is the author of "thelordismyshepherd.com: Seeking God in Cyberspace" and contributor to the children's book, "I Have Some Questions About God." His articles and essays have appeared widely, and his column, "On One Foot," has appeared regularly in The New York Jewish Week since 1994. Rabbi Hammerman was a 2009 winner of the Simon Rockower award, the highest honor in Jewish journalism, for his columns on the Bernard Madoff case. He has been president of the Interfaith Council of Southwestern Connecticut and the Stamford Board of Rabbis and is a member of the National Rabbinic Cabinet of the United Jewish Communities, a chaplain for the Stamford Police and member of the pastoral advisory committee of Stamford Health Systems.

Rabbi Ari Hart is an Orthodox rabbi and leader of multiple initiatives that bring the Jewish community and the world together to make positive social change. Rabbi Hart co-founded of Uri L'Tzedek (Awaken to Justice): The Orthodox Social Justice Movement, the Jewish Muslim Volunteer Alliance, and launched Or Tzedek, the teen institute for Jewish social justice. A contributor to the Jerusalem Post, Haaretz magazine, and the Forward, and others, he was recently selected by the Jewish Week as one of the 36 "forward-thinking young people who are helping to remake the Jewish community." He received his ordination from Yeshivat Chovevei Torah in New York City.

Rabbi Lauren Grabelle Herrmann is the founding rabbi of Kol Tzedek Synagogue, which is reviving Jewish life in West Philadelphia for a new generation of seekers. Rabbi Lauren, a 2006 graduate of the Reconstructionist Rabbinical College, is committed to integrating spiritual practice and social justice. She is currently on the board of UCGreen, a local greening initiative and is active in POWER, Philadelphians Organized to Witness Empower and Rebuild, which is affiliated with the PICO National Network.

Rabbi Jill Jacobs is the Executive Director of T'ruah: The Rabbinic Call for Human Rights, and the author of *There Shall Be No Needy: Pursuing Social Justice through Jewish Law and Tradition* (Jewish Lights 2009) and *Where Justice Dwells: A Hands-On Guide to Doing Social Justice in Your Jewish Community* (Jewish Lights 2011). Rabbi Jacobs has been named to The Jewish Daily Forward's list of 50 influential American Jews (2006 and 2008), to The Jewish Week's first list of "36 under 36" (2008), and to Newsweek's list of the 50 most influential rabbis in America (2009, 2010, 2011).

Rabbi David Kaiman serves as the rabbi of Congregation B'nai Israel in Gainesville, Florida. Rabbi Kaiman spent twenty years as a business executive before his rabbinic education at The Jewish Theological Seminary. You can find links to his blog at www.shalomkaiman.com and twitter @DavidKaiman

Rabbi Daniel Kahane is a teacher at Chabad of Aventura, FL. He is the co-author of "The Kabbalah of Time: Revelation of Hidden Light Through the Jewish Calendar."

Rabbi Michael Adam Latz was ordained by Hebrew Union College in 2000. He is the Senior Rabbi of Shir Tikvah Congregation in Minneapolis which thrives in the vibrant intersection of Jewish spirituality, justice, and study. He's married to Michael Simon & they are proud dads of two daughters, Noa & Liat.

Rabbi Sheldon Lewis was born in Chicago and educated at the University of Chicago and the Jewish Theological Seminary in New York City, where he received his rabbinic ordination. He was a student of Professor Abraham Joshua Heschel and has been active in civil and human rights causes, traveling to the FSU on several occasions on behalf of Soviet Jewry. He served as a US Army chaplain after ordination and spent a year in Vietnam. He is rabbi emeritus of Congregation Kol Emeth in Palo Alto, which he served for thirty-three years. He was deeply involved in interfaith work to promote pluralism, mutual respect, and common cause; and he has been equally committed to nurturing bonds among the streams of Jewish expression. He has had an abiding interest in reconciliation efforts in the Middle East as a supporter of the Open House in Ramle, the Al Amal School near Bethlehem, and Rabbis for Human Rights. He is past president of the Northern California Board of Rabbis, among other positions in the Jewish and interfaith communities. He is married to Lorri, and they have been blessed with four sons, three daughters-in-law and six grandchildren.

Rabbi Nina H. Mandel is the rabbi of Congregation Beth El in Sunbury, PA and an adjunct lecturer at Susquehanna University. She serves on the Executive Committee of the Reconstructionist Rabbinical Association.

Pastor Michael McBride is pastor of The Way Christian Center in West Berkeley and director of the PICO National Network's Lifelines to Healing Campaign, a faith-based effort to reduce gun violence.

Rabbi Joseph B. Meszler is the spiritual leader of Temple Sinai of Sharon, Massachusetts and the author of several books and articles, including: "Facing Illness, Finding God: How Judaism Can Help You and Caregivers Cope When Body or Spirit Fails" (Jewish Lights Publishing 2010), "A Man's Responsibility: A Jewish Guide to Being a Son, a Partner in Marriage, a Father and Community Leader" (Jewish Lights, 2008) and "Witnesses to the One: the Spiritual History of the Sh'ma" (Jewish Lights, 2006). Rabbi Meszler also taught as an instructor during the summer of 2002 at the Smithsonian Institution Resident Associates program on the DC National Mall. He was ordained at Hebrew Union College in Cincinnati in 1999.

Rabbi Jack Moline is the rabbi of Agudas Achim Congregation in Alexandria, Virginia. He also serves as Director of Public Policy for the Rabbinical Assembly and as an adjunct faculty member of the Jewish Theological Seminary and Virginia Theological Seminary.

Rabbi Jesse M. Olitzky is Assistant Rabbi at the Jacksonville Jewish Center in Jacksonville, Florida. Working with all age groups, he is passionate about helping individuals, not just learn Torah, but live Torah as well. Committed to social justice, action, and advocacy, Rabbi Olitzky believes that as God's creations, we must actively work to make God's vision of peace a reality.

Rabbi Jack Riemer is the co-editor of *So That Your Values Live On* and the chair of the National Rabbinic Network, a support system for rabbis across all the denominational lines. He is a former consultant to President Bill Clinton.

Rabbi Julie Schonfeld was named the Executive Vice President of the Rabbinical Assembly (RA), the international association of Conservative/Masorti rabbis, in 2009. The RA supports the professional work of rabbis, promotes an inspiring approach to Jewish tradition, and brings forward the vision of the Conservative/Masorti rabbi in areas including major liturgical publications, public policy, Israel advocacy, social justice, and interreligious affairs. Prior to being named Executive Vice President, she was Director of Rabbinic Development at the RA, spearheading projects in areas such as social justice, conversion, rabbinic conduct, mentorship and women's' advancement. Rabbi Schonfeld serves on President Obama's Council for Faith-Based and Neighborhood Partnerships; in addition, Newsweek recently named her one of the 50 most influential Rabbis in America and she was named by Jewish Women International as a "Woman to Watch" in 2011. She has also been named in the Forward 50.

Rabbi Ronit Tsadok is a Rabbinic Fellow at Ikar in Los Angeles. Her road to the rabbinate included fundraising at Rutgers University, retail at Target, and teaching at Solomon Schechter Day School in New Jersey. Ultimately, she was inspired to become a rabbi and share her love of Torah, justice, and tradition with the masses.

Rabbi Sam Weintraub is a graduate of Haverford College and received Rabbinic ordination from the Jewish Theological Seminary of America. He has been spiritual leader of Kane Street Synagogue, in Brooklyn, New York since 1996. His most recent Jewish achievement is founding the Open Beit Midrash at Kane Street, a weekly gathering of several dozen students, of all ages, who share dinner, study Torah together, and enjoy live new Jewish spiritual music.

CPSIA information can be obtained
at www.ICGtesting.com
Printed in the USA
LVOW01s1312150716
496484LV00022B/410/P

9 781482 333817